Key Account Management

Key Account Management

Building on Supplier and
Buyer Perspectives

Malcolm McDonald and Diana Woodburn

FINANCIAL TIMES

PRENTICE HALL

Cranfield
UNIVERSITY
School of Management

PEARSON EDUCATION LIMITED

Head Office:
Edinburgh Gate
Harlow CM20 2JE
Tel: +44 (0)1279 623623
Fax: +44 (0)1279 431059

London Office:
128 Long Acre, London WC2E 9AN
Tel: +44 (0)171 447 2000
Fax: +44 (0)171 240 5771
Website: www.business-minds.com

First published in Great Britain 1999

© Cranfield University, The Cranfield Marketing Planning Centre,
Cranfield School of Management 1999

The right of Malcolm McDonald and Diana Woodburn to be identified as authors
of this work has been asserted by them in accordance
with the Copyright, Designs, and Patents Act 1988.

ISBN 0 273 64426 2

British Library Cataloguing in Publication Data
A CIP catalogue record for this book can be obtained from the British Library.

10 9 8 7 6 5 4 3 2 1

Typeset by Boyd Elliott Typesetting
Printed and bound in Great Britain

The Publishers' policy is to use paper manufactured from sustainable forests.

About the authors

Professor Malcolm H.B. McDonald MA(Oxon), MSc, PhD, FCIM, FRSA is Professor of Marketing Strategy and Deputy Director, Cranfield School of Management with special responsibility for external affairs.

He is a graduate in English Language and Literature from Oxford University, in Business Studies from Bradford University Management Centre, and has a PhD from Cranfield University. He has extensive industrial experience, including a number of years as Marketing Director of Canada Dry.

During the past twenty years he has run marketing seminars and workshops in the UK, Europe, Japan, India, the Far East, Australia, South America, South Africa, Brazil and the USA.

He has written twenty-eight books, including the best-seller, *Marketing Plans: how to prepare them; how to use them*, and many of his papers have been published. He is Chairman of the Editorial Board of the *Journal of Marketing Practice: Applied Marketing Science*.

His current interests centre around the use of information technology in advanced marketing processes.

Diana Woodburn BSc, MSc, MBA, MCIM, Chartered Marketer is Director of Marketing at The Marketing Process Company. She is a marketing strategy consultant specialising in key account management, a subject on which she is a visiting lecturer at Cranfield University School of Management.

She has a first class honours degree and a Masters degree in biological chemistry. Diana worked in market research in the agricultural chemicals industry before moving into market development and product management in various sectors in Australia, Africa and the Middle East.

Returning to European markets she worked in the fields of office products, consumer goods and mobile communications before becoming a marketing consultant.

Diana developed the Chartered Institute of Marketing's benchmarking assessment for marketing processes through to a unique software-based system. She has worked for such companies as Shell Chemicals, Texaco, Laporte Industries, BOC, Marks & Spencer, Acco Rexel, Oracle and The Post Office.

Contents

List of figures

List of tables

Cranfield School of Management Research Reports Series

The Cranfield School of Management Research Reports series is a major new initiative from Cranfield School of Management and Financial Times Prentice Hall.

The series combines the best in primary research from one of the world's foremost management schools with the traditional publishing and marketing skills of Financial Times Prentice Hall. The reports are designed to allow senior managers to apply the lessons from this research to their own organisations in order to promote best practice across a range of industries.

For further information on other titles in the series, please contact Financial Times Prentice Hall on + 44 (0) 1704 508080.

Editorial board

Foreword

Internationalisation and market maturity have led to increased customer concentration and power, which in turn have led to an unprecedented interest in account management. But, this time around, it is different. Organisations are beginning to realise that Key Account Management is not the area sales manager type activity of old, a post to which successful sales people were promoted as a reward step in their sales careers.

Today, organisations are beginning to appreciate the advantages that can be gained from rationalising their supplier base and are increasingly demanding global, seamless service from them in the quest to gain both economies of scale and competitive advantage.

The problem is that suppliers are not organised to deal with their customers in this way and, as they turn to the academic community for guidance and advice, they find something of a black hole, for Key Account Management (KAM) had never really made it to the realm of scholarly respectability so coveted by university business schools around the world.

This began to change in 1994 with the ground-breaking research of Professor Tony Millman and Dr Kevin Wilson who, *inter alia*, developed a model which explored and better explained a range of relationships moving from pre-KAM to synergistic KAM.

In 1996, using Millman and Wilson's work as a basis to test and develop their theories by exploring best-practice Key Account Management, the Cranfield School of Management set out to publish a preliminary, qualitative survey entitled *Key Account Management: Learning from Supplier and Customer Perspectives*. The title was important, because the study was one of the very few that took a dyadic approach. In other words, we were as keen on hearing the customer's view as the supplier's view, and were surprised to uncover a number of myths surrounding this erstwhile sales-oriented domain. This report was widely read and the associated Cranfield course attracted thousands of delegates from blue-chip companies around the world.

This encouraged us to continue the research, for it is clear that there is still an enormous amount of confusion surrounding Key Account Management, such as how key accounts are selected and classified, how objectives and strategies are set, how profitability is measured, what skill sets are required, how people are motivated and rewarded, how companies should be organised and so on. Accordingly, we formed a Key Account Management Best Practice Club at Cranfield and this particular report is the first publication emanating from it.

We decided that it would be sensible to do a quantitative survey to check out some of our earlier qualitative findings. The work was carried out by a very skilled manager and researcher, Diana Woodburn, with whom Cranfield is fortunate to be associated. It is Diana Woodburn who has done most of the work, including data analysis and preparation of this report, and I should like to thank her for her patience and diligence.

Fortunately, the findings of this quantitative survey confirm and build on our earlier research. Diana is now engaged on the third, in-depth qualitative stage of our research programme and I expect to be able to publish the next research report in 1999.

My thanks, therefore, go to Diana Woodburn, of the Marketing Process Company.

Finally, let us not forget that, as in all complex domains, it is the pioneers and thought-leaders who provide the opportunity to advance learning. In the domain of Key Account Management, the work of Millman and Wilson stands out like a beacon. It contributed a model and new insights that enabled Cranfield to make the kind of further advances documented in the 1996 report and in this one, and scholars and practitioners will remain grateful to them for providing the foundations on which others have been able to build.

Professor Malcolm McDonald
Professor of Marketing Strategy

Acknowledgements

The authors would like to thank the following people for their input into this project, whether by providing the information on which this project is based, recruiting respondents or offering valuable contributions and comments on the report:

- respondents who completed questionnaires, from companies across a wide range of sectors, who will be anonymous;

- respondent recruitment: Shamrock Marketing;

- additional contributions: John Leppard, for general discussion and particularly for Figure 5.5;

- Bernard Gracia, European Institute of Purchasing and Supply;

- review of draft report: John Leppard, Dr Andrew Myers, Dr Hugh Wilson, Dr Frank Fishwick.

Executive summary

INCREASING MARKET TURBULENCE

The increasing globalisation of business means greater pressures and opportunities than ever before. Market turbulence is increasing apace: suppliers can lose huge volumes of sales very quickly now that global customers can choose from any one of a range of global sources; failure in one country's economy sends shock waves throughout the rest of the world; new technology constantly changes the competitive landscape and yet real operational effectiveness is often still an illusion as systems grow ever more complicated. In the midst of this turbulence, suppliers – and customers also – seek to develop closer relationships to reduce their exposure to risk.

Some suppliers have discovered that they have retained the customer, but at a cost which turns the business into a loss.

KEY RELATIONSHIP FOCUS

The management of relationships with key trading partners has become a focal issue in many companies over the last few years, but there are still many questions outstanding about how they should be handled and by whom. New risks have been identified: for example, some suppliers have discovered that they have retained the customer, but at a cost which turns the business into a loss. Cranfield School of Management, in this and previous research, is seeking to find the means of analysis by which companies can interpret their position within key relationships, and to develop models which can help diagnose and support sound strategic directions.

ROLE OF QUANTITATIVE RESEARCH

The Key Account Management (KAM) research project reported here is based on a quantitative survey. Much of the preceding research on the subject has been qualitative and often anecdotal, and it seemed time to substantiate and underpin it, or interrogate it, with a study conducted across a wider base of companies. In doing so, the different nature of the data, its usefulness and limitations should be recognised. Nevertheless, the study has confirmed some important tenets in KAM, and formulated new models to help in understanding this complex and important area of business.

FUNDAMENTAL QUESTIONS

The fundamental question for companies must be 'If we develop our relationships with customers, will we increase our profits?' This question cannot be answered simply, and needs to be broken down into elements which are more answerable, such as 'How can we tell what stage of development each customer relationship has reached?' 'Are closer relationships necessarily more successful than more distant ones?' and 'Are closer relationships more profitable, in the short term and longer term?'

UNIVERSALLY APPLICABLE RELATIONSHIP TERMS

In order to compare relationships across different companies and sectors, this study developed a scheme to characterise each relationship and allocate it to a universally applicable, labelled category. New labels are proposed (and have already been adopted in Cranfield's teaching) which describe the relationship itself. Both buying and selling companies can now use the same terms to talk about the situation between them, which is, after all, the same entity, albeit seen from different angles. Adoption of these labels as common terminology would facilitate discussion of the issues between experts in supply chain management and key account management. These new labels were confirmed with members of the Cranfield KAM Best Practice Club as being more accurate bi-partite descriptions of the relationships than those originally used by Millman and Wilson in their early 1990s ground-breaking research.

Proposed names for the five stages of relationship (or six, if 'disintegrating' is also counted as a stage) are as follows:

1. *exploratory* : searching and matching, before serious trading commences;

2. *basic* : 'no frills', emphasis on efficient transactions;

3. *co-operative*   :   more than strictly transactional, positive but not close;

4. *interdependent*   :   recognition of mutual advantage, frequent contact and dialogue;

5. *integrated*   :   rare type, joint activity, cross-boundary teams, development of trust;

6. *disintegrating*   :   transitional stage of regression or exit, can start from any level.

JOINT STRATEGIC PLANNING

The relationships investigated in the survey were the two or three largest in each company, and this effectively excluded stages other than *co-operative*, *interdependent* and, rarely, *integrated*. In relationships of this size and importance, joint strategic planning might have been expected to be standard practice: it was not, only occurring in about a third, but it was a significant difference between *co-operative* and *interdependent* relationships. Joint strategic planning requires time and effort, and it is symptomatic of *co-operative* relationships that they do not get this level of attention.

EXCLUSION FROM DEVELOPMENT OPPORTUNITIES

Compared with *interdependent* relationships, *co-operative* ones provide selling companies with less access to staff in most of the buying company's functions. Selling companies in this situation appear to receive less information and, in particular, are mostly excluded from product/service development: this contrasts with *interdependent* relationships, where three-quarters of selling companies are involved. Involvement in product/service development is a golden opportunity to design out product cost to mutual advantage, to guide development away from supplier weak points, and to get the customer to buy into the supplier's specification.

Joint strategic planning might have been expected to be standard practice: it was not.

SUCCESS

If there were no connection between success and closer relationships, there would be no point in investing in them. A link was found between relationship stage and perception of the relationship's success, albeit not a simple one. In a majority of cases, higher perceptions of success were associated with *interdependent* rather than *co-operative* relationships. *Interdependent* relationships are also more successful if measured in terms of the buying company's category spend.

Selling companies' views tend to be overoptimistic.

A substantial minority does not conform to this 'rule'. Where the relationship is unsophisticated and successful, it may well be appropriate to the buying company's needs and provide a satisfactory return for the selling company, which is holding on to its gross margin rather than seeing it leak away in providing excessive service. Where the relationship is sophisticated and unsuccessful, it could be that the cost of the sophisticated relationship is not properly accounted for. Indeed, in some relationships large amounts of gross margin were swallowed up in customer services. The business may be retained, but perhaps at a punishing cost.

CAUTION: SUPPLIER DELUSIONS

More relationships were viewed as highly developed by selling companies than by buying companies. Since there are two parties to a relationship, it cannot proceed further than the more reluctant participant will allow. It follows that selling companies' views tend to be overoptimistic, and studies of key relationships in the supply chain need to take account of this bias. Selling companies should allow for the phenomenon when taking decisions in the light of their internally derived analysis of their position with customers.

NEW CONCEPTUAL MODELS

KAM positioning

The KAM relationship should sit squarely in between the selling company and the buying company. A new model shows KAM relationships in this position, interfacing with both companies' processes and their products/services. They are also affected by the strategy of each company, very much at the level of strategy which is actually implemented. Finally, these elements are influenced by the external and internal environments of each company, all of which are included in this model (section 5.1).

Hierarchy of KAM relationships

The potential progression of KAM relationships can be depicted as a pyramid in which each relationship should reach a level of need satisfaction without which it cannot expect to achieve the next stage. The model suggests that each stage contributes further dimensions to the relationship, which are in addition to, not instead of, the dimensions of the lower stage. The needs of the parties to KAM relationships are likened to those of the individual in parallel with Maslow's hierarchy, equating physiological needs with efficiency of transactions and self-actualisation with fulfilment of the potential of the two companies together rather than as separate entities. The pyramid also reinforces the corroborated suspicion that the incidence of each type of relationship decreases as relationship development increases (Section 5.2).

Contact mapping

The survey studied the amount of contact between selling and buying company and which functions were involved. The results are mapped onto Porter's value chain models of the companies. This approach highlights the large difference in communication for companies in co-operative relationships compared with interdependent ones. The weight of communication is clearly visible as much less in the former, who tend to be kept out in the cold and, consequently, in the dark (Section 5.5).

The needs of the parties to a relationship are likened to those of the individual in Maslow's hierarchy.

NEXT STEPS

This study supports and extends understanding of the important topic of key account management. Quantitative information has its uses, particularly its objectivity, which discourages presumption of conclusions; at the same time, it has limitations. Association of factors may be proved, but cause and effect is not. The format is also rather rigid for an extremely complex subject, which has an impact across several functions and levels within both buying and selling companies and is currently in a state of flux as well. The next stage of research will therefore be qualitative in order to probe deeper and wider within each company, albeit involving fewer in the sample. Interviewing started in the summer of 1998.

1

Introduction

1.1 PROJECT CONTEXT

KAM drivers

The amount of interest shown in Key Account Management has grown in recent years from the academic point of view as researchers and luminaries appreciate the scope and complexity of the subject, and from the practical business point of view as pressures of globalisation, new technology in production and communication, economic turbulence and ever-accelerating marketplace dynamics demand new responses.

Reducing exposure to so much risk through the development of better relationships is becoming increasingly important. Morgan and Hunt (1994) suggest, 'To be an effective competitor (in the global economy) requires one to be a trusted co-operator.' Since Cranfield started its research in this field (McDonald, Millman and Rogers, 1996), a considerable number of companies have shown a real thirst for greater insight into Key Account Management, almost amounting to desperation in some cases.

The bulk of published research has been almost exclusively qualitative and based on very small samples, some studies covering only one buyer/seller trading pair or 'dyad'. This type of investigative research has exposed the complexity of the subject, but there is much work still to do to establish models and cause/effect linkages which can be applied in analysis or planning.

Ever-accelerating marketplace dynamics demand new responses.

Research design

This research project took a quantitative route, in an endeavour to establish some simple facts in Key Account Management to support and strengthen (or challenge) current understanding, which includes logical assumptions and intuitive and conceptual developments, as well as findings from smaller-scale qualitative studies. The aim of the study was to test the robustness of some of the foundations of KAM theory, rather than to develop further insights for which in-depth interviews with two-way interaction would be required in a subject of this scope and complexity.

The study focused on the relationship between selling and buying companies and the characteristics and manifestations of it. A scheme was

Practitioners may wish to read section 1.2 and then move straight to Chapter 4 (Results) or even Chapter 5 (Discussion).

used to determine the stage of development of the relationship, which was applied in examination of the differences between the stages. The study addressed key questions in relationship characterisation and success, which should interest companies that are making crucial decisions on how best to deploy their resources in Key Account Management.

As expected, discussion of the research findings raises speculation on a number of issues which cannot be settled by quantitative analysis. These issues will be investigated in Cranfield's ongoing programme of research into Key Account Management, through working interactively with world-leading companies and through a further qualitative research project. In recognition of the far-reaching effects of these important relationships within both the selling and buying organisations, this new phase of research will investigate the views of functions outside the immediate point of contact between key account manager and purchasing manager, and involve people in order processing, logistics and finance, for example. Interviewing started in summer 1998, and the report is expected to be available in late 1999.

This report begins with a short summary of the KAM relationship stages described in Cranfield's earlier research project (McDonald, Millman and Rogers, 1996) in section 1.2: the reader should be acquainted with the contents of this section before embarking on the rest of the report. The brief literature review which follows aims to put this quantitative survey into a balanced perspective, taking into account previous scholarly research on the subject (Chapter 2). The methodology used to collect the information is then explained in some detail (Chapter 3). Reporting of the results (Chapter 4) is separated from, and followed by, a broader-based discussion and extension of their meaning and implications (Chapter 5). Conclusions are drawn throughout this discussion section, and therefore the formal conclusions (Chapter 6) are brief and top-level.

The report is written in the normal, tried and tested, academic format. Practitioners may wish to read section 1.2 and then move straight to Chapter 4 (Results) or even Chapter 5 (Discussion), and refer back if they wish to understand the origin of the conclusions in greater detail.

1.2 KAM RELATIONSHIPS

KAM relationship labels

As frequent reference is made to the different stages of KAM relationships throughout this report, they are briefly described below together with the models developed by Millman and Wilson (1994) and researched further in McDonald, Millman and Rogers (1996). In their original paper, Millman and Wilson proposed a set of names for different stages of development of key account relationships, which are shown in Figure 1.1 in italics. Clearly, in discussions of complex subjects like Key Account Management, recognised terms are needed to describe bundles of attributes which are used frequently. Even if there is a general recognition that these terms are only a form of shorthand, they should be as accurate as possible in order not to mislead or misrepresent the complex situation behind them.

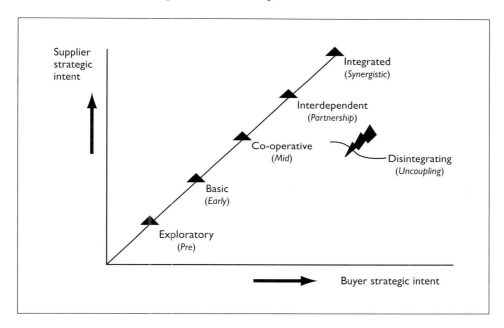

FIGURE 1.1

KAM relationship labels (developed from Millman and Wilson, 1994, with their original labels in italics)

The names used by Millman and Wilson (1994) and by McDonald, Millman and Rogers (1996) were a mixture of labels, with various origins. One described how the two parties might view the relationship (*partnership*), another described an aspect of the relationship (*synergistic*), and others contained an implication that stages of the relationship are dependent on time or some other natural progression (*pre*, *early*, *mid*). In fact, although progression from one relationship stage to the next is quite possible, it is by no means automatic. In certain circumstances, it may not be appropriate for relationships to become closer and more sophisticated; in other cases, one of the parties may not want to take the relationship further.

Although trading partners may progress through the stages of relationship sequentially, it is also possible to enter any of them directly. Similarly, if the relationship fails, any stage can be exited directly or gradually, depending on circumstances.

Relationship stages are shown at equal intervals along the axes, but there is no reason to suppose that they would take equal amounts of time to reach; indeed, that is most unlikely. Unless some particularly significant event or shift occurs, developing relationships will change by degrees, so the labels should be applied to a range of states of relationship, rather than to a single, precise specification.

Many of the alternative labels (some of which are discussed in section 2.4) are names which reflect the perspective of either the selling company (e.g. *prospective*) or the buying company (*preferred supplier*). Given that there are two parties to each relationship, and that the subject of study is the interaction between the two, it seems logical to apply labels which describe the relationship itself. The new set of labels as proposed below is used throughout this report. They were discussed with the Cranfield KAM Best Practice Club, whose members approved this platform for labels and accepted the new versions as appropriate in their view.

KAM relationship descriptions

The essence of each stage of KAM is described below, while the development of contact between buying and selling companies is discussed in greater detail in the original report by McDonald, Millman and Rogers (1996) and therefore only briefly mentioned here.

Exploratory KAM

This stage, illustrated in Figure 1.2, precedes Key Account Management of any kind, but implies that the potential importance of the relationship will qualify the buying company as a key account if business is secured. At this stage the selling company will be courting the buying company and exploring its needs, which of them they are required to fulfil, the size of the opportunity, and generally getting a feel for the organisation, the people who are influential in the buying decision, their personalities and modus operandi. At the same time, the buying company with a need will be exploring the supplier's offer, capabilities and credentials, quite possibly with more than one supplier simultaneously.

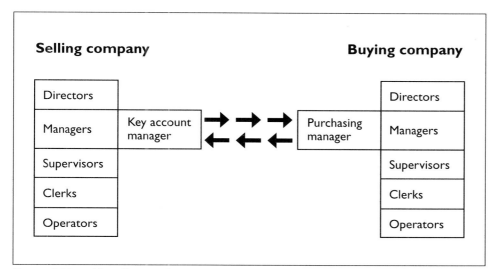

FIGURE 1.2

Exploratory KAM relationship

(*Source*: McDonald, Millman and Rogers, 1996)

Basic KAM

This stage implies a relationship with very much a transactional emphasis. If it is a new relationship, then it may be effectively a trial time, during which the selling company has to prove its ability to deliver its offer in an efficient manner. Buyers will obviously prefer to develop business further with suppliers who have demonstrated that they can live up to minimum operational requirements. However, trial experience of each other may not always be possible, e.g. major contracts. At this stage, the buying company may also use other suppliers of the same product/service, but not necessarily: multiple sourcing may not suit the need.

Even if the relationship is successful at this level, it may still not be appropriate to develop it for a number of good reasons, for example:

- there may be changes pending in the environment in terms of legislation, technology, market, company ownership, etc. which limit the length of life of the relationship, so that investment in relationship building is unlikely to pay back;

- the buying company may be low-cost focused and unresponsive to added value;

- the buying company may be known for supplier switching;

- in summary, the overall lifetime value of the relationship is not expected to repay investment in the relationship in terms of time, adaptation, etc.

As described in the earlier research, most contact will be one-to-one through the key account manager and the purchasing manager (*see* Figure 1.3).

FIGURE 1.3

Basic KAM relationship

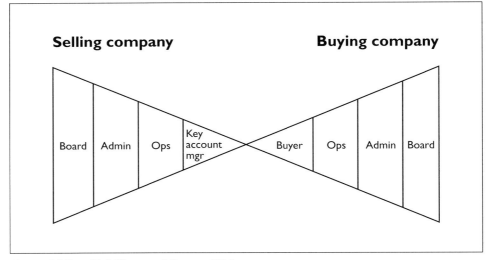

(*Source*: McDonald, Millman and Rogers, 1996)

Co-operative KAM

At this stage the buying company may have been able to satisfy itself about the selling company's credentials through its own experience after a period at basic KAM level. If performance is acceptable, the selling company may then be able to work more closely with the buying company and develop the relationship. Opportunities to add value to the customer will be suggested by the supplier, and the buyer will adopt a positive and communicative attitude towards the supplier, perhaps in terms of indicating further opportunities to do business together or helping the supplier to solve some of the operational problems which arise.

If the customer uses a list of preferred suppliers, the selling company will be on it but, as mentioned above, it is not necessarily appropriate for some kinds of purchases. Contact involves a wider range of people. It is often at this stage that the real potential to progress the relationship from co-operative to interdependent is either grasped, or not, by the supplying company as, by definition, the relationship is already more complicated than at the basic stage (*see* Figure 1.4).

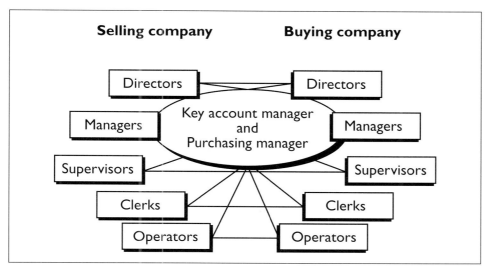

FIGURE 1.4

Co-operative KAM relationship

(*Source*: McDonald, Millman and Rogers, 1996)

Interdependent KAM

At this stage, both buying and selling company acknowledge the importance of each to the other. They are locked into each other, not inextricably, but if the relationship were to end, retreat would be difficult and time-consuming. Inertia, as well as strategic suitability, holds the partners together. They may have set up various initiatives together, like common working practices, product specifications, joint marketing activity, etc. which would take time and effort to undo.

Even if multiple sourcing is possible in theory, in fact the selling company has become sole or at least first-option supplier. A range of functions in both organisations work closely together, orchestrated by rather than administered by or channelled through the key account manager and purchasing manager (*see* Figure 1.5).

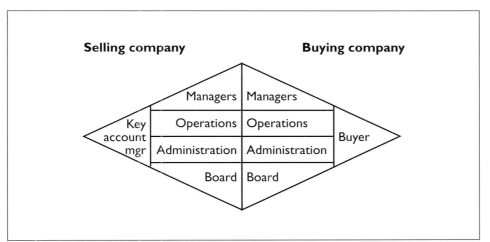

FIGURE 1.5

Interdependent KAM relationship

(*Source*: McDonald, Millman and Rogers, 1996)

Integrated KAM

This type of relationship involves working together in cross-boundary functional or project teams (*see* Figure 1.6). By this means the organisations become so integrated that individuals may feel more affinity with their team than with their official employer organisation. The teams run the business, rather than either of the organisations, and they make decisions about their interactions with other teams according to the strategy they are implementing. They may even be based at their partner's premises.

Exit would be traumatic at both a personal and organisational level.

FIGURE 1.6

Integrated KAM relationship

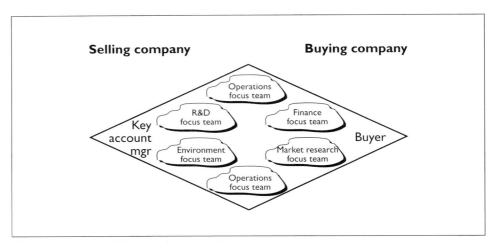

(*Source*: McDonald, Millman and Rogers, 1996)

Disintegrating KAM

At any time, the relationship can fall apart for one or more of a large number of reasons, such as a takeover of either company, a change of key people, a switch to a new supplier offering better products, performance or price, or the introduction of new technology. Disintegration can be sudden and exit complete, or it may mean a return to a lower level of relationship at which the companies can continue to do business together but on different terms. In any case, disintegrating KAM is not a stable state, as any of the others can be, but a transitional stage before the relationship settles down into another stage, possibly no relationship at all.

The key account manager's role may change to damage limitation, and a business developer may not be the right kind of person to fulfil this need.

2

Background

2.1 DEFINITIONS

Key accounts

McDonald, Millman and Rogers (1996) defined key accounts as 'customers in a business-to-business market identified by selling companies as of strategic importance'. This definition immediately begs the question of how strategic importance should be defined in this context. In practice, key accounts are effectively defined by the criteria used by selling companies to select them. The criteria used, albeit sub- or semi-consciously, commonly relate to a mixture of size (current and potential) and complexity. Pardo, Salle and Spencer (1995) point out that much of the literature confirms that companies largely take definition/selection for granted.

Many companies still list huge numbers of customers as key accounts. If they genuinely embraced the idea that realisation of Key Account Management, as opposed to competent major account management, implies development of rather intense and far-reaching relationships, they would recognise the need to ration the number of candidates for this treatment. That recognition would then drive prioritisation and more rigorous selection, which would finally result in a tighter definition of key accounts.

Some authors have taken the key account concept beyond the bounds of customer relationships to include internal and lateral relationships as well: Morgan and Hunt (1994) identified ten types of partnership in companies. However, this discussion will confine itself to buyer/supplier relationships. Two types were identified in each case: 'ultimate' and 'intermediate' buyers (Anderson and Narus, 1990), both of which may be included in the definition of key accounts; and 'goods' and 'services' suppliers. The latter distinction may be somewhat outmoded: in recent years many products have been heavily augmented with services, and services have been rendered into almost tangible products, so that separation of the two groups is hardly meaningful in many aspects of business discussion. It may be more useful to divide inputs into elements for resale, after value-adding (i.e. included in cost of sale) and elements for consumption by the business itself (i.e. included in overheads).

Customers in a business-to-business market identified by selling companies as of strategic importance.

Key Account Management

Burnett (1992) defines Key Account Management as 'the process of allocating and organising resources to achieve optimal business with a balanced portfolio of identified accounts whose business contributes or could contribute significantly or critically to the achievement of corporate objectives, present or future'. From this definition, global account management is a specific subset within Key Account Management, to which similar principles may be applied, but which also has its own particular characteristics. National (or key) account management has also been defined as an approach in which one executive or team takes overall responsibility for all aspects of a customer's business, directly or co-ordinating the activities of others (Shapiro, 1989).

An approach in which one executive or team takes overall responsibility for all aspects of a customer's business.

Although Key Account Management is a process conducted by selling companies with customers, it is notable that neither of these descriptions mentions selling. Indeed, in many cases where the relationship has been in existence for years, if not decades, the customer is already 'sold', and the emphasis has switched to management and development across a broad front. This change of emphasis has important implications in the definition of the role of key account managers.

Burnett's interpretation is a logical extension of McDonald, Millman and Rogers's (1996) definition of a key account, except that the implications of the word 'balanced' should be considered. Depending on what kind of balance is envisaged, it may be that a company maintains balance across its entire customer portfolio, but not necessarily within its key account portfolio. Key accounts should, for example, be defined by strategic importance, which implies other characteristics as well.

Key account manager

The key account manager could simply be defined as the person who enacts the process of Key Account Management. According to Burnett's definition, that would be at the highest level at which decisions are made for the company's whole portfolio of customers. In normal parlance, however, a key account manager's role is more closely allied with Shapiro's description: he or she is directly attached to specific key accounts, which may be a small (in number) portfolio of customers, or may be only one customer.

Definitions of the Key Account Management process are clearly important in defining the way the role should be fulfilled and the skills required to be successful in it. Definition of the role of the key account manager will continue to evolve, at least as long as understanding of the processes is still evolving. For example, the selling company's strategy for the customer and the nature of the relationship are major factors affecting the demands on the key account manager's role. Relationship models developed in earlier research (McDonald, Millman and Rogers, 1996: *see* section 1.2) demonstrate visually the different stages of sophistication and affinity which selling and buying companies may achieve, linked with the different roles for the key account manager at each stage. Although these models demonstrate the differentiation between the nature of the role in principle, there is still much to be learned about it in practice.

Whether the Key Account Manager operates by control or persuasion is an important issue.

Companies have tried a range of formulae for the definition of roles between the key account manager and field salesforce, who are often required to play an important part in implementation (Cohen, 1996). The situation is paralleled by that of global account managers *vis-à-vis* country managers or national account managers. Whether the key account manager operates by control or persuasion is an important issue. Yip and Madsen (1996) conclude that global account management has proved very successful for global players, but that cultural differences are such that it would be dangerous to work on a world-wide control basis, and the role should be one of persuasion and co-ordination.

Degree of control is only one of the several factors relating to the selling company's inability to implement which have caused Key Account Management programmes to founder. In fact, Key Account Management more often fails because of the selling company's organisational problems in delivery of the programme (Stevenson, 1981) than the buying company's inability to accept it or deliver a satisfactory return to the selling company (although that is common as well). As an example, Citibank's global account management programme was highly effective with customers, but was nevertheless successfully sabotaged by country managers (Buzzell, 1985); it was eventually revived, though some time later.

The breadth of the organisations involved must be considered alongside the breadth of activity demanded by the selling company. One has only to contemplate the vastness of some of the customers and the extent of their companies in terms of industry sector and geography, which is often matched by a similar situation in the selling company, to see how the management of interaction between the two organisations dwarfs the simple idea of selling. Logically, if the role is not defined as selling, then perhaps salespeople, in general, should not fulfil it.

2.2 ORIGINS OF KEY ACCOUNT MANAGEMENT

Sales origins

The concept of Key Account Management has several parents. Undoubtedly, its name is derived from the sales function, and many relevant papers have been published under titles such as national accounts, major accounts and strategic customer alliances. At the leading edge of both academic and applied thinking, it has largely outgrown its sales origins, but there are still manifestations of more traditional thinking leading to continuing controversy over the nature and status of the role. For example, in the UK the NVQ level of key account manager was fixed at level 4 in line with field sales manager (Millman and Wilson, 1996).

If the role is not defined as selling, then perhaps salespeople should not fulfil it.

Selling has always been characterised by reward structures different from any other function in the organisation. It has been widely accepted in practice that powerful financial incentives should be offered and directly linked to short-term outcomes, usually sales volume, occasionally margin. On this motivational principle has grown up a whole culture and ethos in and around selling and salespeople that will not readily be changed, neither in organisations that have trusted to it for decades, nor with salespeople who have operated in this environment for their entire career.

Although 'old-style' approaches to selling may not be appropriate in the context of key accounts, new approaches need to address the drivers which made traditional practices popular in the first place (Cohen, 1996). They will also need to address the legacy and remnants of traditional practices for the foreseeable future. Some authors on sales topics are still recommending heavily commission-biased remuneration for any account, though others have accepted that real Key Account Management will not be achieved while it is still linked with this fundamental tenet of selling (Francis, 1998; Boles, Barksdale and Johnson, 1996). In fact, it may be that the remuneration framework is the litmus test that sets apart genuine key account managers from salespeople of all seniorities, and is ultimately the distinguishing factor that indicates where Key Account Management is really conducted as much more than a sales role.

Relationship marketing

Key Account Management may be seen as part of the newer discipline of relationship marketing. Although definitions of relationship marketing vary, most refer to relationships with customers, e.g. 'relationship marketing concerns attracting, developing and retaining customer relationships' (Berry and Parasuraman, 1991). Morgan and Hunt (1994) went further to include all kinds of commercial associations, not just customers, in their definition: 'Relationship marketing refers to all marketing activities directed towards establishing, developing and maintaining successful relational exchanges.'

However, Key Account Management does, by definition, confine itself to relationships with the customers of supplying companies. Obviously, the viewpoint of those customers is highly pertinent, and indeed approaches like transaction cost analysis have provided a useful theoretical framework for examining business-to-business relationships (Williamson, 1985; Pfeffer and Salancik, 1978). Commercially, a substantial stream of relationship marketing now focuses on developing the application of information technology to marketing and developing customer intimacy on a one-to-many basis. This situation is far more typical of the consumer environment, where marketing may be targeting millions of people, than of business-to-business sectors, where the numbers are usually smaller. It is not really relevant to Key Account Management, which is intended to be focused on just a few selected customers.

It may be that the remuneration framework is the litmus test that sets apart genuine key account managers from salespeople.

Supply chain management

Although still called Key Account Management, much of this new discipline should be about the relationship itself, which is intrinsically bipartite. However, most of the literature originates from either the selling

Independence from suppliers was seen as desirable by buyers, until global competition began to force a rethink of traditional stances.

side or the buying side, rarely from a combination of both (Olsen and Ellram, 1997). Research from the 'other side' is very illuminating for both academics and practitioners in Key Account Management.

The complementary discipline of supply chain management has much to contribute to an even-handed and objective understanding of the potential of these key relationships. Buying companies operate supply chain management principles to gain the benefits of vertical integration and the advantages of outsourcing simultaneously. They will be seeking to achieve advantages such as competitive pricing, additional expertise and flexibility, and avoid the disadvantages frequently encountered with internal, group suppliers, for example high fixed cost, lack of flexibility and complacency.

In the past, independence from suppliers was seen as desirable by buyers, until global competition began to force a rethink of traditional stances in favour of greater collaboration and mutual dependence (Scott and Westbrook, 1991). Supplier opportunism is probably their greatest fear, but as the number of examples of successful collaborative relationships grows, more buyers should become convinced of the viability of the approach. Ellram (1991) describes the supply chain management approach as 'aimed at co-operatively managing and controlling distribution channel relationships for the benefit of all parties involved, to maximise efficient use of resources in achieving the supply chain's customer service goals'.

A group of European researchers, the IMP Group (from the International Marketing and Purchasing study), developed a model, as shown in Figure 2.1, using an interaction approach to buyer/seller relationships which was based on transaction cost analysis and inter-organisational theory (Ford, 1990; Håkansson, 1982). Originally it focused on the co-operative aspects of the relationship without taking into consideration the competitive elements of business relationships, of which all of those directly involved are well aware. This may have been an over-reaction to stark economic theory, which is heavily based on competitive behaviour (Alderson, 1965), and the model has since been modified to acknowledge these intrinsic attributes of business relationships.

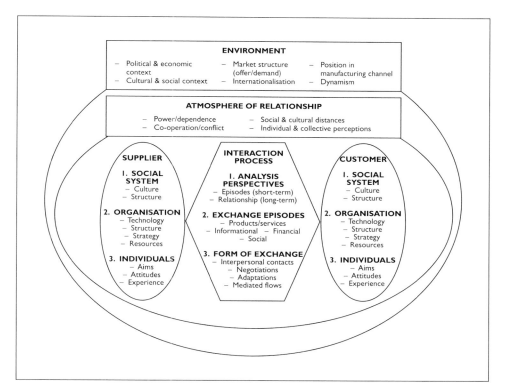

FIGURE 2.1

The International Marketing and Purchasing (IMP) Group model

(*Source*: Turnbull and Valla, 1986)

2.3 BENEFITS OF KEY ACCOUNT MANAGEMENT

Benefits can include the possibility of collaboration in real mould-breaking strategies.

Risk reduction

Clearly there are potential benefits from Key Account Management or companies would not be energetically engaged in pursuing this approach. Theoretically, the benefits to the selling company are business growth, risk reduction and possibly cost reduction; however, as discussed below, there is a danger of uncontrolled cost increase as well. On the buying side, the impetus towards further development of supplier relationships is mainly driven by cost reduction and risk reduction (*see* Table 2.1 for a list of sources of benefit under each of these two headings), leading to enhanced customer satisfaction and contributing to overall competitive strategy. Benefits can include the possibility of collaboration in real mould-breaking strategies which challenge the supply map status quo in order to bypass competition, and which a buying company cannot achieve alone.

TABLE 2.1

Types of risk reduction and cost reduction for buying companies originating from partnership with selling companies

Risk reduction	Cost reduction
Sharing of assets (lower breakeven costs)	Reduced production costs
Sharing of information, informally and formally	Reduced transaction costs
Increased flexibility versus vertical integration	– better information/reduced uncertainty
Volume commitments	– routinised transactions
Future orientation with joint planning	
Trust	
Interdependence	
Sharing of risks and rewards of relationship	

(*Source*: Ellram, 1991)

Although key accounts have the potential to deliver the greatest profit, they also have the potential to generate the greatest losses.

Both parties benefit from risk reduction, which must be a major driver in relationship development. 'Internal' risks may be considered as being of two kinds: short-term crises such as sudden demand or supply gaps, and longer-term uncertainties which complicate planning and result in sub-optimal use of resources. External risks are those originating in the market, or originating outside the market and acting through it, as in the case of government legislation, for example.

These two types of risk may be related to the two types of interaction identified in the IMP model (Håkansson, 1982): episodes, defined as short-term events that contribute to institutionalising or destabilising the interaction (Ford, 1980), and relationships, the long-term exchanges that take place. A collaborative relationship has the potential to reduce external risk for both parties through market information sharing, greater flexibility in response and leveraging market influence, for example.

Financial drivers for selling companies

Building and maintaining relationships at a sophisticated level has considerable costs: Yip and Madsen (1996) listed a number demanded by global account management, most of which apply to management of other types of key account as well. Nevertheless, selling companies expect the direct financial benefit to outweigh the relationship costs. An increasing body of evidence points to the greater profit to be gained from retaining existing customers, compared with finding, attracting and establishing new customers (Bain Customer Retention Model, 1990).

However, although key accounts have the potential to deliver the greatest profit, they also have the potential to generate the greatest losses. Recent studies (e.g. Wilson, 1997) have shown that it is often a company's largest two or three customers that lose money when costs are fully attributed to them. Good, appropriate information systems and the will to use them, plus careful management, are needed in order to ensure financial benefits from key accounts. Loss situations often arise when the buyer has negotiated a price based on the cost of goods sold, but is enjoying excess value in terms of a range of additional, uncosted services. One of the major dangers in developing sophisticated relationships through Key Account Management is the escalation of costs absorbed by and in the relationship.

There is an additional danger that sophisticated and close relationships are seen as the only formula in Key Account Management. In fact, there are many cases of customers who should still qualify as key accounts, who should be managed within an efficient, transactional relationship. They may not want to develop the relationship further, or the business may not be able to repay investment in it. Analysis of each key account should focus on the *incremental* benefit of investing in development beyond its current status.

Cost savings for buying companies

There are 'legitimate' or mutually beneficial cost savings available to buying companies that are preferable to driving suppliers' profits below adequate levels. Better management of the flow of supplies, elimination of unnecessary or duplicated processes and tighter quality control all reduce cost. Several authors have reported on case studies illustrating the cost benefits available; in fact, Marks & Spencer is an example which predates by decades the formulation of the concept of supply chain management (Scott and Westbrook, 1991).

Better management of the flow of supplies, elimination of unnecessary or duplicated processes and tighter quality control all reduce cost.

In addition to savings in current operational costs, savings through collaborative product development and R&D cost sharing are a very significant source of advantage, particularly to companies with high investment in development, long development cycles or markets with short product lifecycles. The buying company benefits from supplier expertise, leading to better and more cost-effective design, while the selling company can beta-test new products or services in real life on a larger scale than their own facilities permit.

There are potential dangers attached to close relationships for buying companies as well. The range of pitfalls may be grouped around two issues: cost increase (from duplication of effort and/or from the substitution of cash for activity, by giving the supplier the opportunity to add some of the value that the buying company could have fulfilled itself) and control/dependence concerns (Ellram, 1991). Paradoxically, concerns about the negative aspect of dependence may be seen as an outcome derived from positive, ongoing relationship benefits when considered together with the issue of termination costs. In fact, the latter may originate more from setting up an alternative than exiting the current relationship, so it is debatable whether such costs should be looked at as a barrier to exit.

All these fears are paralleled by selling companies, except that concern about price/margin erosion replaces concern about cost increase. The issue of dependence may be slightly different, but is very real if the relationship accounts for a large proportion of the selling company's turnover.

2.4 KEY RELATIONSHIP DEVELOPMENT

Relationship stages

Millman and Wilson (1994) distinguished a typology of relationship development stages. They identified six, and gave them the following labels:

- pre-KAM: the searching/prospecting stage;
- early KAM: based on transactional exchanges;
- mid-KAM: where preferred supplier stage was achieved;
- partnership KAM: multi-function and multi-level communications;
- synergistic KAM: with close integration into functional teams;
- uncoupling KAM: as the relationship disintegrated.

McDonald, Millman and Rogers (1996) described these further in their research among 13 seller/buyer dyads.

However, for reasons described in section 1.2, these labels have been replaced in this report with a new set which, as agreed with members of the Cranfield KAM Best Practice Club, are more appropriate descriptors of a dyadic relationship, having acknowledged the Millman and Wilson antecedents.

Other authors have reported a similar progression (Ford, 1980), albeit each has given them different names and concentrated on different elements of their characterisation. A common thread is the change from a transaction-based, functional relationship to a partnership approach. Dunn and Thomas (1994) identified four stages:

- transaction selling: reactive, order-focused, tangible item;
- product solution: augmented products, higher-level sell;
- business solution: linked product solutions, typically project buying situation;
- partnership solution: multiple business solution to address strategic problem.

However, this characterisation seems to omit some common buying situations which are normally included in such schemes of relationship development. For example, there seems to be no reason why transaction selling has to relate to a tangible item rather than, say, to a simple service. The stage called 'business solution' appears only to represent projects for application to the business, but there are relationships at a similar level which may involve the supply of components or materials into the customer's ongoing production process. A relationship which permits the development of creatively conceived processes for delivery of the product, for example closely dovetailed with those of the customer, has also reached this level.

'Deconstructed' firms are emerging which rely on co-ordinated relationships with other firms to provide non-core value chain activities.

Buyer/seller relationships do not exist in a vacuum but may be regarded as part of a business network (Anderson, Håkansson and Johanson, 1994). To a certain extent, all dyadic relationships are part of a network, but some networks have been specifically designed to serve the needs of the supply chain through a more creative or lateral approach than traditionally. Anderson et al. noted that 'deconstructed' firms are emerging which rely on co-ordinated relationships with other firms to provide non-core value chain activities. They also stressed the importance of considering the dyadic relationship as the prime focus, albeit embedded in a network.

Transaction cost influence on relationship development

A substantial body in the literature pursues the understanding of buyer/seller relationships through transaction cost analysis, as demonstrated in the model in Figure 2.2 (e.g. Lohtia and Krapfel, 1994;

Olsen and Ellram, 1997). Transaction cost analysis acknowledges real situations by assuming that information required for decision-making is normally incomplete and, in addition, that participants on either side of the relationship may be opportunistic and hold back, or misrepresent, information that they could contribute.

FIGURE 2.2

Transaction-specific investment benefits model

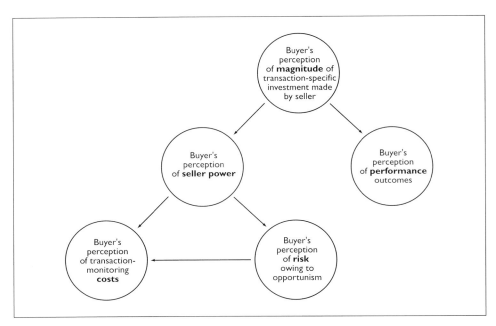

(*Source*: Lohtia and Krapfel, 1994)

Transaction costs can be reckoned as being of two types: investments and ongoing operational costs. Transaction-specific investments are those invested in the relationship that cannot be recovered on breakdown (e.g. customer/supplier-specific assets, time spent on relationship development), and ongoing costs are the time and money spent in monitoring the relationship to protect the company's interests and manage uncertainty.

In theory, relationships should develop in ways that seek to reduce transaction costs or secure profit from transaction-specific investment. These analyses are not easily completed, but anyway it seems that relationships are not invariably developed according to the rationale this theory would indicate. There are other approaches to understanding why relationships have arrived at their current stage, which look at power and commonality of interest (*see* below) and a range of other factors (Olsen and Ellram, 1997). Nevertheless, the approach is a useful alternative or adjunct to the IMP model.

Relationship portfolio analysis

Companies will probably be involved simultaneously in relationships of all types. There will be various reasons why each has reached that particular stage. There will also be different opportunities within each that should determine what, if any, action should be taken to develop the relationship further. In the same way that the GE (General Electric) or directional policy matrix plots a company's portfolio of market segments against their strength in the market, key accounts can be analysed in order that appropriate strategies can be applied for each of them.

Fiocca (1982) looked at key accounts in this way, and others have taken similar approaches (Olsen and Ellram, 1997). In particular, McDonald and Rogers (1998) point out that key customers are not all equally attractive, nor is the selling company always in a strong position. Strategies should differ, not only according to what the selling company would like to achieve, but also according to what is realistically possible and accepted by the customer, while taking into account the strategy for the market segment overall (*see* section 5.3).

Relationship management mode should be selected according to the relationship type and the company's perception of its position of power within it.

Krapfel, Salmond and Spekman (1991) also portray different relationship types derived from a portfolio analysis approach. Their descriptive scheme draws on the use of strategic indicators including transaction cost analysis, plus political economy, resource dependence and relational contracting, to characterise the nature of an appropriate relationship in each case. Their scheme uses relationship value and interest commonality to arrive at four relationship types (*see* Figure 2.3). The appropriate relationship management mode, they suggest, should be selected according to the relationship type and the company's perception of its position of power within it, provided that it is matched by the other party to the relationship. The nature and compatibility of strategies on the part of both buying and selling company are also highly relevant in deciding the level to which relationships should be developed.

In the previous section, the benefits of closer relationships were discussed, but these can only be realised within the context of the environment and atmosphere of the relationship (Ford, 1980). The IMP model identified the normal environmental factors and a set of four elements which determine the relationship atmosphere: power/dependence, co-operation/conflict, trust/opportunism and social distance.

FIGURE 2.3

Relationship mapping model

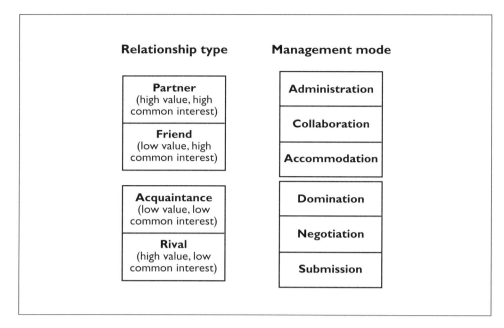

(*Source*: Krapfel, Salmond and Spekman, 1991)

In effect, two major streams of approach to the examination of buyer/seller relationships are discernible: one focusing on the more qualitative and positive aspects of the relationship, in which interaction variables such as commitment and trust play a large part (e.g. Morgan and Hunt, 1994) and in which the IMP model plays a pivotal part; and the other focusing on more quantitative aspects and acknowledging potentially negative aspects such as exercise of power, which is based around variables such as transaction costs and resource dependence. Neither, of course, is oblivious to the alternative point of view, and there is considerable overlap between the two schools of thought.

This necessarily brief review of previous scholarly research in this domain has provided a backcloth to the current initiative and has guided this study. Many aspects of this quantitative survey and its interpretation were guided by the work of earlier researchers.

3

Methodology

3.1 SURVEY STRUCTURE

Quantitative versus qualitative

A large proportion of the research on Key Account Management to date has consisted of qualitative studies (e.g. Anderson, Håkansson and Johanson, 1994; Dunn and Thomas, 1994), and therefore covered small numbers of companies. Some papers have researched just one example in considerable depth (e.g. Pardo, Salle and Spencer, 1995).

Given the complexity and novelty of the subject, qualitative research is a good option for expanding and deepening understanding of the topic, as it includes the opportunity to probe and confirm findings through dialogue. However, there also appeared to be a need to validate and confirm on a broader front the indications gained from these small-scale studies. Hence the decision to continue investigation through quantitative research at this stage.

Sample company size and role

Previous studies have predominantly researched only one side of the buying/selling relationship, either the selling company in Key Account Management, or the buying company in supply chain management. For this study, the view was taken that to examine the relationship objectively, both sides would need to be consulted. It was thought unlikely that sufficient self-completion questionnaires for both sides of the same relationship would be achieved. However, the methodology adopted included both buyers and sellers, so that common differences in views would be collected.

Although many smaller companies exhibit excellent Key Account Management, some of the issues which are of great importance do not arise in the same degree and nature, for example problems of organisational complexity, multiple roles in the market, pressures of globalisation. The turnover minimum was therefore set at £100 million per annum, which will have tended to exclude cases where the relationship is driven by the power which derives from an imbalance in company size. It also excludes cases where small companies can use their speed and flexibility to develop good relationships with larger ones. In fact, many of the companies responding proved to have a turnover much lower than £100 m because, even though they belonged to a large group, they were run as separate small business units (SBUs). A study of the link between relative size, the exercise of power and the development of the relationship would be another project in itself.

Finally, in order to ensure a good spread of company characteristics and market influences, companies were also sampled according to their position in the supply chain, i.e. manufacturer, distributor or retailer. An original intention to sample on the additional dimension of products versus services proved difficult to apply in practice; many companies sell both, and do not accept this parameter as a genuine differentiator as most products are now heavily augmented with services.

Sample structure

Table 3.1 shows the structure of the sample quotas to which companies were recruited. The breakdown for buying companies and selling companies is not the same only because retailers did not qualify as selling companies for the purposes of this project, in which key accounts are defined as business-to-business customers. For various reasons, the actual sample profile was somewhat different (*see* section 3.2), though still well balanced and wide-ranging.

TABLE 3.1

Quotas proposed for sample recruitment by role in survey and role in market

	Buying companies %	Selling companies %
Manufacturer or service provider	16	26
Reseller/distributor/wholesaler	16	26
Retailer (buying side only)	16	0
Total	48	52

3.2 QUESTIONNAIRE

Pilot

The questionnaire was designed for self-completion (*see* Appendix C). It was piloted with seven respondents, from both selling and buying companies, for questionnaire formulation and time to complete. After the pilot stage, it was possible to tell participants in the full survey that it should take about 25 minutes to complete. The main difficulty reported by respondents was the unambiguous definition of the unit on which the survey was based: group, operating company, division, etc. As different companies are constituted differently, it was difficult to specify a universal unit. In fact, there would be little point in asking people questions to which they did not know the answers, so the pragmatic solution had to be the business unit that was recognisable to the respondent.

The definition of the company unit was therefore clarified, particularly for the purposes of questions relating to size of turnover and other values. The wording of the questions for selling companies on margin and contribution was also clarified. It was accepted that some companies would not be prepared to disclose financial information when approached in this way (and possibly any other).

Questionnaire administration

The questionnaire was mailed to named respondents who had been qualified by telephone as being the most senior person in the company responsible for key account managers or purchasing managers. It was sent with a stamped addressed envelope and covering letter explaining the nature of the project, thanking participants for their help and promising a copy of the survey report when produced.

The questionnaire was divided into two main sections: a section of questions about the company contacted, and a section of questions about specific trading partners. As respondents in the pilot study, particularly selling companies, had wanted to detach certain parts of the questionnaire to be completed by different people, the sections were physically separable. Two versions of the questionnaire were developed, one for selling companies and the other, more or less a mirror image of the selling company version, for buying companies. The wording was changed to be appropriate to each case, and the selling company questionnaire also included questions on customer margins and contributions which were not asked of buyers. The two surveys were merged for analysis.

Selling companies were given three copies of the second section and asked to complete one for each of their three largest customers, and buying companies were given two copies of their second section and asked to complete one for each of their two largest suppliers. The difference in number requested reflected the difference in support expected: because of the survey's title and content, it was thought that input would be easier to gain from selling companies than from buying companies. In the event, this proved not to be the case, but this method meant that, in the final composition, the numbers of relationships reported by selling companies was very close to the number reported by buying companies (47 and 42 respectively).

Questions were mostly precoded. Many of them were five-point Likert scales, with parameters grouped around particular aspects of KAM relationships. To gain a summary of each aspect, scores on each parameter were totalled as well as being reported separately. Scoring schemes are shown in Appendix B.

3.3 SAMPLE RECRUITMENT

Respondent selection

Suitable companies were identified from a broad-based list of UK companies in frequent use.* Companies were contacted by telephone, and their activity in the market ascertained (manufacturer etc.) and the name of the most senior person responsible for Key Account Management or supply chain management, as appropriate.

If possible, contact was made with the person named, but in many cases they were not contactable, and the assurance of their secretaries or assistants was accepted where given. In the event, many of these assurances of participation proved unfounded.

In order to give some urgency to completion, a return date was added to each, depending on the date of telephone contact. The survey was conducted in the last quarter of the year, which turned out to be a particularly busy time during which many people were very involved in budgets and leave. In retrospect, addition of the date probably acted more as a disincentive to completion than the incentive it was expected to be, because some people who did not complete the questionnaire in the given time then discarded it on the assumption that their reply would be too late.

---

* Supplied by Shamrock Marketing, Chesham.

Response

Of 300 companies that were contacted, 37 companies replied (12 per cent). They completed the survey questions for 89 key account relationships in total. Of these 89 relationships, 47 were reported by 16 selling companies and 42 by 21 buying companies. Although more buying companies than selling companies actually participated, the balance in the survey was maintained on this dimension because they contributed approximately equal numbers of relationships.

The spread of companies is shown in Table 3.2, classified by their role in the market. There is a degree of double-counting in this table (17 per cent) because some companies reported dual roles, e.g. as both manufacturer and distributor. However, the analyses used in the rest of this report do not depend on this breakdown.

The category of service provider is shown separately to represent a service originator and a service distributor: in many cases it was not realistic to make a distinction between them, and service provider is a term commonly used to cover both or either.

A further demographic description of the sample is given in greater detail in Appendix A. Overall, a good spread of activity and sector was achieved, and a greater spread of size in some respects, as some of the operating companies belonging to large groups had relatively small turnovers themselves.

Base:	Buying companies 21		Selling companies 16	
	No.	% of total	No.	% of total
Manufacturer	7	19	10	27
Service provider	8	22	5	14
Reseller/distributor/wholesaler	5	14	3	8
Retailer	5	14	0	0
Total	25	68	18	49

TABLE 3.2

Breakdown of actual sample by role in survey and role in market

3.4 ANALYSIS

Validity checks

The appropriateness of individuals completing the questionnaires is an important factor in confirming the validity of survey results. In this case, the job title profile of those who did reply is shown in Appendix A, section A.3. The level of respondent is considered good overall, and appropriate for the questions asked. In several cases where the questionnaire was passed on to someone other than the person to whom it was addressed, the first contact made a point of explaining that the respondent had been selected as more appropriate and knowledgeable in this area. As mentioned in section 3.2, in some cases they took the trouble to divide the questionnaire among the people who would be best able to answer it.

Of respondents who had agreed to participate, or for whom agreement had been given by their staff, but failed to return a questionnaire, a large proportion was telephoned to ascertain reasons for non-response. A mix of explanations was given, but no real patterns emerged in terms of reasons or respondents, and indeed a few additional questionnaires were received as a result of the call-back. It is therefore concluded that non-response is not a source of bias in the sample achieved.

Level of confidence

The results were analysed on Snap Professional software. Statistical significance was generally tested by chi-squared values. Results shown were mostly significant at the 1 per cent level,[1] occasionally at the 5 per cent level and in one case at the 10 per cent level, and this is made clear in the text. Confidence levels and chi-squared values[2] are noted throughout the report, close to the appropriate information. In all cases where appropriate, tables have been truncated to ensure that expected frequencies are better than 5, so that these statistical tests are valid.

Nevertheless, we regard the survey as exploratory. It should be remembered that Key Account Management is a very complex subject, and respondents' interpretations of the wording of the questions can vary across the wide range of different circumstances in which they were answered. The breadth of companies involved does, on the one hand, offer protection against bias towards the situation in any particular sector or group of sectors but, on the other hand, it also means that some respondents may be trying to answer questions formulated in a way that is hard to apply in their circumstances.

Therefore, even where the results show a high level of significance as reported, they should, like any other results, be interpreted in the light of common sense and other sources of understanding of the subject. This was the approach used in writing Chapter 4, and it should be read in the same light.

NOTES

1. Where a result is given as being significant at the 1 per cent level, it means that the difference between the measurement (of behaviour, attitude or whatever) between one group and another is real, and that there is only 1 chance in 100 that this could have occurred randomly. The reader can then have confidence in the finding, because there is only a small chance of its being wrong. Similarly, significance at the 5 per cent level means that there is a larger chance of its occurring at random rather than in reality, but still only 1 in 20, which is usually considered satisfactory. Where the confidence level is 10 per cent, or 1 in 10, of being found at random, it is still ten times more likely to be a real phenomenon rather than 'accidental', but should perhaps be treated as provisional rather than proven.

2. Chi-squared values indicate the degree of difference between the actual findings and what could have been observed if answers had occurred at random and there were no patterns of difference between breakdown groups. So that positive and negative differences do not cancel each other out, the differences are squared; chi-squared values are the sum of the squares of the differences. A minimum theoretical value can be computed for each level of confidence which will depend on the number of groups or degrees of freedom. If the observed chi-squared value is greater that that computed, the reader can be sure that observed behaviour (attitude etc.) differs from random behaviour. In all cases where the chi-squared value is given, it is greater than that for the appropriate degrees of freedom, and confirms the level of confidence that can be placed in the result.

4

Results

4.1 STAGE OF RELATIONSHIP DEVELOPMENT

What describes the nature of KAM relationships?

The stage to which a relationship has developed will be characterised by the behaviours and beliefs or attitudes of the parties engaged in it. Question 7 therefore offered respondents a set of statements about the behaviours and beliefs in each relationship (Figure 4.1) with which they could agree or disagree on a five-point scale. The statements related to dimensions which Millman and Wilson (1994), McDonald, Millman and Rogers (1996), Dunn and Thomas (1994), Morgan and Hunt (1994) and Pardo, Salle and Spencer (1995), among other authors, had identified as likely to change as relationships developed.

FIGURE 4.1

Statements offered to respondents to indicate stage of relationship development

Question 7 *To what extent do you agree or disagree with the following statements, applied to your relationship with this supplier/buyer?* (Answered on Likert 5-point scale)

Barriers to exit (mutual dependency)

'If either company (us or our supplier/customer) ever wanted to end our relationship, both companies would find it difficult and complicated to exit.'

Competitor monitoring (trust)

'We/they still monitor competitors regularly to check up on their/our performance.'

Partnership (approach)

'There is a real spirit of partnership between our two companies.'

Cross-functional teams (internal orientation)

'Looking after our/their business is not just the responsibility of the key account manager: both companies have set up cross-functional teams of people dedicated to meeting our/their needs.'

Joint strategic planning (commitment)

'Together we have planned and formally documented long-term strategies for the development of our relationship.'

Social association (personal relationships)

'We keep our relationships with the people in this customer's/supplier's organisation strictly on a business footing: we don't meet outside work.'

Respondents were asked the extent to which they agreed or disagreed with each statement as it applied to their relationship with the customer/supplier they had nominated. The score total was compared with expected answers for the different stages of KAM relationship (*see* Appendix B, Table B.1). Each relationship was then allocated to a KAM development stage on this basis. Some statements were posed in reverse (i.e. agreement is negative, disagreement is positive as far as closer KAM relationships are concerned) in order to avoid habitual answering patterns, and the scores also reversed accordingly.

How are KAM relationships split between co-operative and interdependent?

Table 4.1 shows the distribution of relationship scores overall. In fact, only one relationship fell into the 'basic KAM' category; but as respondents were asked about their largest/most important customers/suppliers, this should not be surprising. However, in spite of this bias towards what should be the best, only one relationship fell into the 'integrated KAM' category, suggesting that this closeness of association is quite rare.

TABLE 4.1

Stage of development of KAM relationship analysed by viewpoint

Total score on KAM relationship statements	Total relationships	Viewed by supplier	Viewed by buyer
Base:	89	47	42
6–18 co-operative/basic*	46	18	28
	52%	38%	66%
19–30 interdependent/integrated*	43	29	14
	48%	62%	33%

* Only one relationship of this type found

See Appendix B for description of scoring framework.

Chi-squared value = 7.15.

Significant relationship at 1% level.

The remaining relationships were more or less evenly divided between scores representing 'co-operative KAM' and 'interdependent KAM'. Such a result may mean that market circumstances dictate that this is the right level of relationship in each case. However, although that will undoubtedly be the case in some instances, it may also indicate that the level of achievement of close relationships is not high because KAM is a poorly developed process in many companies.

Selling companies will probably be more concerned about this lowish overall level of relationship development than their customers. Selling companies are likely to feel more vulnerable at the early stages of the relationship than buying companies, especially when they have invested in setting up the relationship and have not yet recouped their investment.

In fact, the real position for selling companies may be worse than at first sight: buying companies seem to see KAM relationships as less developed than do selling companies (*see* Table 4.1 – bearing in mind that the sellers and buyers in this survey were not describing the same relationships).

So the overall average is probably biased by a certain amount of unwarranted optimism and wishful thinking by sellers who believe they have a closer relationship with their customers than the latter recognise. Logically, the reality of a relationship is the minimum level of engagement that is acknowledged by both parties and therefore the optimistic view must be discounted if it exists on one side only.

Bearing in mind this bias, which cannot be removed without resorting to objective, multi-function and cross-border interviewing, this framework is used as a regular analysis of responses in this survey to examine how the stage of development of the KAM relationship might affect other expressions of it. Relationships will be divided into two groups: those considered to be 'basic' or 'co-operative' (called 'co-operative' hereafter as only one 'basic' relationship was found), and those considered to have reached 'interdependent' or 'integrated' (called 'interdependent' hereafter as only one 'integrated' relationship was found).

Which elements occur most in successful relationships?

Table 4.2 shows responses to the various KAM relationship stage indicator statements individually. The extent of agreement and disagreement with each is shown overall and according to perceived success of the relationship, which is defined and discussed in section 4.2. The statements are not listed in the order asked, but in order of overall strength of agreement.

Buying companies seem to see KAM relationships as less developed than do selling companies.

TABLE 4.2

Agreement/disagreement with KAM relationship stage indicator statements analysed by KAM success

KAM relationship stage indicator statement	Reaction to statement	Total relationships	Success: quite poor, neither poor nor good	Success: very or quite good
Base:		89	43	46
Cross-functional teams (*internal orientation*)	Agree	65%	52%	79%
	Disagree	(12%)	(17%)	(7%)
	Ave. score	3.66	3.43	3.91
Partnership (*approach*)	Agree	56%	41%	72%
	Disagree	(15%)	(24%)	(5%)
	Ave. score	3.49	3.22	3.79
Social association* (*personal relationships*)	Agree	(24%)	(28%)	(21%)
	Disagree	54%	52%	56%
	Ave. score	3.34	3.24	3.44
Barriers to exit (*mutual dependency*)	Agree	51%	45%	56%
	Disagree	(39%)	(42%)	(37%)
	Ave. score	3.21	3.11	3.33
Joint strategic planning (*commitment*)	Agree	31%	20%	44%
	Disagree	(45%)	(52%)	(37%)
	Ave. score	3.02	2.57	3.51
Competitor monitoring* (*trust*)	Agree	(83%)	(85%)	(81%)
	Disagree	6%	2%	11%
	Ave. score	2.02	1.89	2.16

	Chi-squared values	Level of confidence
Cross-functional teams	7.104	5%
Spirit of partnership	10.406	1%
Joint strategic planning	6.268	5%

Scoring: 5 = strongly agree; 3 = neither agree nor disagree; 1 = strongly disagree.

* Statement posed in reverse, i.e. agreement is negative, disagreement is positive, hence figures in brackets ( ) are negative as far as closer KAM relationships are concerned.

Ave. scores calculated from: (Score × Respondents choosing)/Total respondents. Scores reversed on negative statements, e.g. strong agreement on a negative statement scores 1.

In successful KAM relationships nearly three-quarters adopt a spirit of partnership.

The statement on *internal adaptation*, in terms of setting up cross-functional teams, gained most agreement overall, suggesting that this could be one of the first signs of a key account relationship. Indeed, this kind of adaptation is firmly linked with relationship success. Next most common is the development of a positive *approach*, expressed as a spirit of partnership between companies. In fact, there is a significant difference here between the less successful relationships and those perceived as successful; in the latter nearly three-quarters adopt a spirit of partnership, compared with less than half of the others. Social interaction, which develops as more *personal relationships* grow, is at a similar level overall, and is no different whether the relationship is successful or not.

For about half of relationships respondents agreed that exit would be difficult and complicated, implying recognition of *mutual dependency* at a pragmatic level.

What might be considered to be real *commitment*, expressed in terms of joint long-term strategic planning, is quite limited overall: there was some evidence of occurrence in about a third of relationships. However, there was a strong correlation with successful KAM relationships, where nearly half were involved, compared with only one in five of other KAM relationships.

Some authors have discussed the development of *trust* in the relationship, demonstrated by the customer's ceasing to check up on the supplier by monitoring competitor activity. This research shows that this hardly ever happens, and that nobody is under any illusion about it. Disclosure of information is also an indication of trust, which is examined in section 4.6.

To a large extent, suppliers and buyers see their relationships in fairly similar ways in terms of the order of agreement with these six dimensions of the relationship, and none of the differences shown are individually statistically significant. However, it would be interesting to investigate further to establish whether more sellers than buyers do indeed think that they have reached stages of mutual dependency and personal friendship.

There was a strong correlation between joint strategic planning and successful KAM relationships.

Summary

Six dimensions of behaviour and belief were used to characterise the stage of development of relationships in the survey. Two types dominated: co-operative and interdependent.

Buyers and sellers generally agreed on the order of incidence of the six dimensions. However, buyers reported fewer relationships at interdependent level, suggesting a mismatch of perception between the two sides.

Cross-functional teams were set up in a high proportion of relationships. A spirit of partnership and social association could also be found in a good proportion of relationships. Half recognised mutual dependency, expressed as barriers to exit. Only a third were engaged in joint strategic planning. Trust in terms of cessation of competitor monitoring was almost completely absent.

4.2 SUCCESS OF KAM RELATIONSHIPS

What are the elements of success in a relationship?

In the same way as the development of the relationship was assessed in the previous section, the relationship's success was judged. Question 16 offered a set of statements about elements which were taken to indicate the success of the relationship (*see* Figure 4.2). Obviously, *financial* considerations are extremely important, but there are other considerations as well, such as *operational efficiency* (source of hassle factors), *compatibility of strategic goals* and *ease of doing business together*, which has repeatedly been highlighted by previous research as being of great importance. The *sustainability* or length of the relationship should be real proof of its success (but *see* section 4.4), but the *ultimate judgement* belongs with the managing director, whether or not he or she considers it to be successful in their terms.

FIGURE 4.2

Statements offered to respondents to indicate success of relationship

---

Question 16 *To what extent do you agree or disagree with the following statements, applied to your relationship with this supplier/buyer?* (Answered on Likert 5-point scale)

Financial

'We are very happy with the financial return we get on this customer's business/value we get from this supplier in financial terms.'

Operational efficiency

'Our operational processes (order handling, logistics, documentation, etc.) work seamlessly and cost-effectively with this customer/supplier.'

Strategic alignment

'Our own strategic goals are very different from this customer's/supplier's strategic goals.'

Ease of doing business

'This customer/supplier is rather inflexible and/or disorganised so it is not easy to do business with them.'

Sustainability

'Our relationship with this customer/supplier must be one of the longest in the sector.'

Ultimate judgement

'Our managing director (or equivalent) rates the business with this customer/supplier as extremely successful and one of the most important to us strategically.'

How successful were the relationships surveyed?

Table 4.3 shows the overall success of the KAM relationships in the survey according to agreement with these statements. As would be expected, remembering that these are the organisation's largest customers or suppliers in each case, very few fell into the category of 'poor'. It is notable that, even so, six (7 per cent) were scored low enough to rate as 'quite poor', and all but one of these were rated as such by the selling company. This may be an interesting manifestation of where the balance of power now seems to lie, i.e. with the buyer. Again, five out of six of the relationships considered as 'quite poor' were at the co-operative stage. At the other end of the scale, only one relationship scored enough to qualify as 'very good'.

Score on KAM success statements	Total relationships	Viewed by supplier	Viewed by buyer	Co-operative	Interdependent
Base:	89	47	42	46	43
6–8 (denoted very poor)	0 / 0%	0 / 0%	0 / 0%	0 / 0%	0 / 0%
9–14 (denoted quite poor)	6 / 7%	5 / 11%	1 / 2%	5 / 11%	1 / 2%
15–20 (denoted neither good nor bad)	40 / 45%	14 / 30%	26 / 62%	26 / 57%	14 / 33%
21–26 (denoted quite good)	42 / 47%	28 / 60%	14 / 33%	15 / 33%	27 / 63%
27–30 (denoted very good)	1 / 1%	0 / 0%	1 / 2%	0 / 0%	1 / 2%

Table 4.3
Success of KAM relationship analysed by viewpoint and stage of relationship development

Viewed by supplier v. viewed by buyer:
Chi-squared value for scores 9–20 v. scores 21–30 = 5.68; significant relationship at 2% level.

Co-operative relationships v. interdependent relationships:
Chi-squared value for scores 9–20 v. scores 21–30 = 9.41; significant relationship at 1% level.

Views on the more moderate levels of success varied according to perspective. Selling companies' ratings split 2 : 1 in favour of the equivalent of 'quite good' over 'neither good nor bad', while buying companies reversed the ratio to 1 : 2. Such a result could have one or more of a number of causes, for example:

- optimistic predisposition of sellers;
- predisposition of buyers always to expect more;

- easier for selling company to assess gain from income (but *see* discussion on customer profitability in section 4.11) than buying company to assess advantage from spend.

Taking into account the high level of relationships rated equivalent to neutral or worse, and the absence of all but one at the very successful level, there seems to be plenty of room for improvement. Overall, views of the success of these relationships seem fairly muted, especially as far as buying companies are concerned.

Where this system for scoring relationship success is used to analyse responses in this survey, relationships will be divided into two groups: those considered as neutral or worse, and those considered to be quite or very successful.

Views of the success of these relationships seem fairly muted, especially as far as buying companies are concerned.

Are more sophisticated relationships more successful?

Companies involved in key relationships will no doubt want to know whether investment in the relationship is likely to lead to greater success, in whatever terms they rate success. Table 4.4 shows a different and simplified version of Table 4.3, in which relationship stages are broken down by success scores in order to examine whether more sophisticated relationships do achieve greater success (according to the parameters listed at the beginning of this section).

Table 4.4

KAM relationship stage by KAM success score

KAM relationship stage	Total relationships	KAM success score	
		21–30 *very or quite good*	6–20 *quite poor, neither poor nor good*
Base:	89	43	46
Co-operative	46 52%	15 35%	31 67%
Interdependent	43 48%	28 65%	15 33%

Chi-squared value = 9.405
Significant relationship at 1% level.

Differences between co-operative and interdependent relationships were of a similar order: only a third of co-operative relationships rated as 'quite good' in contrast to two-thirds of interdependent relationships with the same rating. This important link is discussed in section 5.3.

Of the relationships considered to be at the co-operative stage of KAM, twice as many fell into the less successful scoring range as into the more successful range. Of the relationships considered to be at the interdependent stage of KAM, twice as many fell into the more successful scoring range as into the less successful range.

This appears to suggest that a link does exist between success and sophistication of relationship, which is of fundamental importance. If such a link did not exist, then there would be no point in investing in building relationships towards closer levels. However, the table also shows a substantial minority of relationships that do not conform to this 'rule': some are unsophisticated and successful, others are sophisticated and unsuccessful.

Where the relationship is unsophisticated but nevertheless successful, it may well be that both supplying and buying companies are behaving in ways appropriate to the buying company's needs. The selling company should be achieving a satisfactory return, holding on to its gross margin rather than seeing it leak away in providing unnecessary service. Where the relationship is sophisticated and unsuccessful, it may represent the reverse, with neither side properly accounting for the costs of the sophisticated relationship.

KAM relationship stage and success are linked, but there is also a substantial minority of relationships that do not conform to this 'rule'.

Which elements of success are most common?

Tables 4.5 and 4.6 show responses to the statements which make up the score on success, listed in order of degree of agreement. The average scores are quite closely grouped just on the positive side of neutral, but not with much sign of real enthusiasm. There were few significant differences between responses from buyers and sellers or between co-operative and interdependent relationships.

<table>
<tr><td rowspan="2">TABLE 4.5

Agreement/disagreement with KAM success indicator statements analysed by viewpoint</td><td>KAM relationship success statement</td><td>Reaction to statement</td><td>Total relationships</td><td>Viewed by supplier</td><td>Viewed by buyer</td></tr>
<tr><td>Base:</td><td></td><td>89</td><td>47</td><td>42</td></tr>
</table>

KAM relationship success statement	Reaction to statement	Total relationships	Viewed by supplier	Viewed by buyer
Base:		89	47	42
MD/CEO's view (*ultimate judgement*)	Agree	54%	57%	50%
	Disagree	(10%)	(11%)	(10%)
	Ave. score	3.56	3.64	3.48
Different goals* (*strategic alignment*)	Agree	(23%)	(23%)	(23%)
	Disagree	54%	61%	45%
	Ave. score	3.36	3.45	3.26
Difficult/disorganised* (*ease of doing business*)	Agree	(18%)	(9%)	(28%)
	Disagree	48%	45%	52%
	Ave. score	3.37	3.38	3.36
Financial return/value (*financial satisfaction*)	Agree	49%	53%	43%
	Disagree	(32%)	(36%)	(29%)
	Ave. score	3.18	3.17	3.19
Length of relationship (*sustainability*)	Agree	41%	44%	36%
	Disagree	(28%)	(36%)	(19%)
	Ave. score	3.19	3.15	3.24
Seamless processes (*operational efficiency*)	Agree	40%	47%	33%
	Disagree	(30%)	(21%)	(41%)
	Ave. score	3.09	3.26	2.90

	Chi-squared values	Level of confidence
Difficult/disorganised	10.308	1%
Length of relationship	7.554	2.5%

Scoring: 5 = strongly agree; 3 = neither agree nor disagree; 1 = strongly disagree.

* Statement posed in reverse, i.e. agreement is negative, disagreement is positive, hence figures in brackets ( ) are negative as far as closer KAM relationships are concerned.

Ave. scores calculated from: (Score × Respondents choosing)/Total respondents. Scores reversed on negative statements, e.g. strong agreement on a negative statement scores 1.

The *ultimate judgement* and most important success indicator, the MD or CEO's view, scored the highest of any, though still with only about half agreeing with it. Given that the other elements gained lower levels of agreement, this appears to suggest that CEOs have a tendency, surprising to some, towards a positive outlook. Although more interdependent relationships appeared to be thought to receive a favourable judgement from CEOs than did co-operative ones, the difference is not statistically proved.

KAM relationship success statement	Reaction to statement	Total relationships	Co-operative	Interdependent
Base:		89	46	43
MD/CEO's view	Agree	54%	46%	63%
(*ultimate judgement*)	Disagree	(10%)	(15%)	(5%)
	Ave. score	3.56	3.37	3.77
Different goals*	Agree	(23%)	(35%)	(12%)
(*strategic alignment*)	Disagree	54%	41%	67%
	Ave. score	3.36	3.09	3.65
Difficult/disorganised*	Agree	(18%)	(24%)	(12%)
(*ease of doing business*)	Disagree	48%	44%	53%
	Ave. score	3.37	3.24	3.51
Financial return/value	Agree	49%	42%	56%
(*financial satisfaction*)	Disagree	(32%)	(32%)	(33%)
	Ave. score	3.18	3.13	3.23
Length of relationship	Agree	41%	37%	45%
(*sustainability*)	Disagree	(28%)	(32%)	(23%)
	Ave. score	3.19	3.07	3.33
Seamless processes	Agree	40%	35%	46%
(*operational efficiency*)	Disagree	(30%)	(37%)	(23%)
	Ave. score	3.09	2.93	3.26

TABLE 4.6

Agreement/disagreement with KAM success indicator statements analysed by stage of KAM relationship

A proportion of buyers recorded their feeling that their supplier was indeed quite difficult to work with.

Notes: *see* Table 4.5.

Different goals: chi-squared value 7.953; level of confidence 2.5%.

The feasibility of *strategic alignment* gained a relatively high level of agreement, particularly within interdependent relationships. *Ease of doing business* together gained a very similar score overall, with less polarisation between the stages of relationship. Fewer buyers than sellers sat on the fence here and a proportion recorded their feeling that their supplier was indeed quite difficult to work with. If working together is difficult, incompatibility of strategic goals could be a contributory factor.

Even on the crucial success indicator of *financial satisfaction*, only half of relationships surveyed were viewed positively on either side, and a third were considered in a distinctly negative light. This proportion of dissatisfaction was consistent, regardless of role or relationship. As those surveyed were the most important of the organisation's customer/supplier relationships, this should be a real cause for concern and action.

The *sustainability* or duration of the relationship should be proof of its success, and certainly about 40 per cent thought they had one of the longest relationships in the sector. However, a later discussion of the effect of time suggests that relationships are not so simple. Some of the older ones show signs of unresolved decay and dissatisfaction from participants, and some newer relationships are viewed more favourably.

On financial satisfaction, a third (of relationships) were considered in a distinctly negative light.

Response was most negative overall on 'seamless operations' or *operational efficiency* in terms of average score and lowest proportion in agreement. Buyers may have had a strong influence on this result, perhaps because they no doubt bear the backlash from their own organisation of operational supplier problems. It would be understandable if buyers who are having to deal with the hassle of day-to-day problems are more reserved than suppliers about the current value of the relationship.

Response was most negative overall on 'seamless operations' or operational efficiency.

Operational efficiency would be expected to be one of the most basic requirements in a supply relationship, and although the statement was pitched at a fairly high standard, better results might have been expected. The survey seems to have uncovered a substantial source of aggravation.

Summary

Six dimensions of favourable beliefs were used to characterise the success of the relationships in the survey. A few relationships were considered to be poor, mostly from the selling company's point of view. Even though these are the company's largest/most important relationships overall, views of their success seemed to fall short of enthusiastic: only half gained a rating better than neutral.

Operations seemed to be the most common source of negative attitudes, particularly with buyers. Financial satisfaction was not very high either: half were happy to some extent, but a third were distinctly unhappy with the position on this count, which must be one of the most important.

There appears to be a linkage between development of a relationship to a more sophisticated level and success ratings of good rather than neutral/poor. However, a substantial minority did not follow this rule, falling into both categories of co-operative and successful, and interdependent and neutral/poor.

This probably means that closer, more sophisticated relationships are more likely to be successful than more distant ones, but that a close relationship is not the only successful 'recipe', nor does it achieve success automatically. Companies should make sure they have chosen the right relationships to develop, and still monitor them carefully.

4.3 EFFECT OF TIME

How long are KAM relationships?

Table 4.7 shows the spread of duration of the relationships reported in this survey. There appear to be fewer in the 15–19 years category than any other, but as this is preceded by a higher than average percentage, and succeeded by an average percentage, it is probably not a real phenomenon. Overall, the spread of duration is rather evenly divided, with no dropping off at either end of this scale.

Duration of relationship (years)	Total relationships
Base:	76
0–4	15 20%
5–9	13 17%
10–14	25 33%
15–19	8 11%
20+	15 20%

TABLE 4.7
Duration of relationships

There does not seem to be any evidence that relationship development is time dependent.

Do longer relationships become closer?

If relationships developed continuously over time, the longer a relationship had lasted, the more sophisticated it would be. Figure 4.3 shows duration of relationship with KAM stage to look at this hypothesis. In fact, there is no statistically significant relationship between the two. There was no significant relationship proved between duration and relationship success either.

Logically, there must be an initial minimum period during which the relationship settles down and proves itself, but there does not seem to be any evidence that thereafter relationship development is time dependent, at least once it has endured beyond 'take-off'. It should also be noted that the survey found interdependent KAM relationships less than five years old, and co-operative ones which have lasted for over 20 years.

Figure 4.3

Duration of relationship by KAM relationship stage

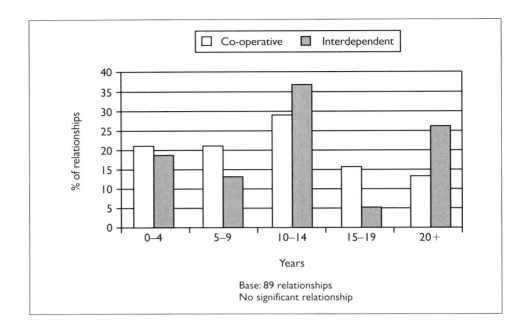

Summary

There is no evidence that time of itself will develop KAM relationships, or that more sophisticated, interdependent relationships necessarily last any longer than co-operative ones.

Equally, there is no evidence that the more successful relationships are longer lived, though presumably a highly unsuccessful relationship would not survive.

4.4 KEY ACCOUNT MANAGER AND KEY RELATIONSHIP NUMBERS

How many key account managers do suppliers allocate to each customer?

Respondents were asked how many Key Account Managers worked on the customer's account. Table 4.8 shows the breakdown of replies by KAM relationship stage.

A substantial number of customers (at least half) are handled by more than one Key Account Manager. This has great potential for confusion, duplication and irritation for the customer, and it would be interesting to know exactly how co-ordination between them works in practice.

Key account managers working in account	Total
Base:	87
1	39
	44%
2	27
	30%
3+	21
	24%
Key account managers from other group companies working in account	32
	36%

TABLE 4.8

Numbers of key account managers

This result suggests that many selling companies are probably still dealing with customers according to their own technical and internal divisions. Alternatively, they may have developed sophisticated communication and co-ordination procedures, but discussions with companies outside this survey indicate that the former interpretation is more likely than the latter. Although all the companies surveyed qualified through claiming to be involved in key account relationships, many have not really grasped the concept of Key Account Management as orchestrated, customer-focused relationship management.

With about a third of customers having key account managers from other companies within the same group dealing with them as well, the potential for duplication of expense and sub-optimisation of effort is enormous.

Analysis by KAM relationship stage and success showed no significant differences.

How many relationships are key to the business?

Respondents were asked how many suppliers or customers they classified as being key to their business (addressed to buying companies and selling companies respectively). Replies are shown in Table 4.9; as the base is rather low, the replies suggest comparisons which cannot be confirmed here.

Many selling companies have not really grasped the concept of Key Account Management as orchestrated, customer-focused relationship management.

TABLE 4.9

Numbers of key customers/suppliers

No. of customers/suppliers classified as key to business	Total companies	Reported by supplier	Reported by buyer
Base:	37	16	21
No reply	2 5%	0 0%	2 10%
0–9	5 14%	5 31%	0 0%
10–19	12 32%	5 31%	7 33%
20+	18 49%	6 38%	12 57%

Chi-squared value = 13.185
Significant relationship at 0.5% level.

A majority, though by no means all, of selling companies seem to recognise that the number that can genuinely be treated as such is limited. One-third have fewer than ten key accounts, and two-thirds in total have fewer than 20 key accounts.

On the other hand, no buying companies at all considered fewer than ten suppliers to be key to their business, and over half had more than 20 'key' suppliers. If this difference is real, it suggests that buying companies are possibly less likely to operate with a key relationship focus than selling companies, and this attitude, if correctly reflected here, may hinder the kind of relationship development which selling companies seek.

How important are key relationships?

If buying companies do not operate with a key relationship focus, that may hinder the kind of relationship development which selling companies seek.

Table 4.10 shows the importance of these relationships in terms of joint share of all sales (selling companies) or purchases (buying companies).

In most companies, all of the relationships they consider to be 'key' together account for over 50 per cent of their sales or purchase budget. However, in half of them, the proportion is still less than 75 per cent. This may indicate that these companies have taken selection further than Pareto's 80/20 rule, or that while the rule may hold in general terms, it is not as extreme as 80/20. Probably both of these hypotheses are true.

Key relationships' share of business	Total companies
Base:	37
No reply	2
	5%
0–24%	4
	11%
25–49%	0
	0%
50–74%	18
	49%
75%+	13
	35%

TABLE 4.10

Key relationships' share of business

Summary

Buyers were roughly equally divided between those with just one key account manager involved in the surveyed relationship, and those with more than one.

In addition, about a third were handled by key account managers from other companies in the same group. This suggests that a good proportion of selling companies have not really grasped the concept of Key Account Management as a co-ordinated, customer-focused process.

Buying companies appeared to count more suppliers as key to their business compared with selling companies' number of key customers. This alone may pose a problem to selling companies trying to develop close relationships: the buying side may be trying to share their energy and resources between a larger number of contenders for attention than does the selling company.

4.5 CONTACT WITH BUYING COMPANY STAFF

How much contact do suppliers get?

Respondents were asked whether suppliers had enough contact with customer personnel, across the range – *see* Figure 4.4.

Table 4.11 shows the results of scoring answers overall according to whether contact with each of these functions was enough, not quite enough or not nearly enough. 'Enough overall' contact on this basis required sufficient contact with a majority of the functions listed, while at the other end of the scale respondents would probably not have recorded sufficient contact with any function.

FIGURE 4.4

Contact between buying and selling company

> **Question 5** *Do your/your customer's people have sufficient contact with the following people in your own company?* (Answered on Likert 5-point scale aggregated to 3 points)
>
> Purchasing manager/main contact
> Order processing/logistics
> Production/technical
> R&D
> Marketing and sales
> Directors

In about half of relationships the situation is satisfactory, and a further third scored a level equating to 'not quite enough'. Around one in ten of suppliers seem to have a real problem with access to the buying company. These cases were reported by buying companies as well as selling companies (data not shown here), so they are not straightforward examples of selling companies being held at arm's length by buying companies.

TABLE 4.11

Overall sufficiency of contact between supplier and buying company functions

Score on sufficiency of contact	Total relationships
Base:	88
Not nearly enough (<10)	10
	11%
Not quite enough (10–14)	32
	36%
Enough (>14)	46
	52%

See Appendix B for means of calculating score.

Does contact differ between co-operative and interdependent relationships?

Figure 4.5 shows that there was a substantial difference between co-operative and interdependent relationships in the amount of customer contact afforded to selling companies (as judged by whether respondents considered it to be sufficient). Although not shown, results based on the success of the relationship were very similar. Selling companies in co-operative relationships are left 'out in the cold' more than those in interdependent relationships.

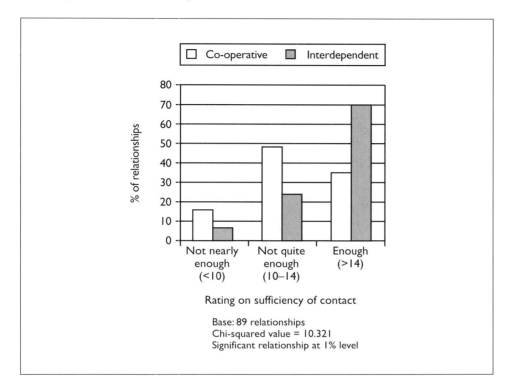

FIGURE 4.5

Overall sufficiency of contact between supplier and buying company functions by KAM relationship stage

Where does contact with buying companies fall down?

Table 4.12 shows the percentages of respondents who considered that there was sufficient contact between supplier and each of the different buying company functions, analysed by relationship stage. There is a high level of sufficiency of contact with the purchasing manager (or other main contact) overall, with three-quarters feeling they have enough contact with this customer function. Two-thirds have enough contact with the operational side, order processing/logistics.

For other functions only about half considered contact to be satisfactory, except for R&D. Contact here was at a lower level, but there may be buyer/seller situations in which contact with R&D is not really relevant anyway. There is still relatively low involvement with the customer's R&D, even though current supply chain management theory suggests that customers could gain substantial benefits through using suppliers' expertise.

Selling companies in co-operative relationships are left 'out in the cold' more than those in interdependent relationships.

TABLE 4.12

Sufficiency of contact between selling company and buying company functions by KAM relationship stage

Contact 'enough' between selling co. and buying co. functions	Total relationships	Co-operative	Interdependent
Base:	89	46	43
Purchasing manager/ main contact	67 75%	29 63%	38 88%
Order processing/ logistics	59 66%	27 59%	32 74%
Production/technical	50 56%	22 48%	28 65%
Directors	50 56%	22 48%	28 65%
Marketing and sales	44 49%	22 48%	22 51%
R & D	32 36%	14 30%	18 42%

	Chi-squared values	Level of confidence
Purchasing manager/main contact	6.198	2.5%

Interdependent relationships generally seem to achieve more satisfactory contact across the board when compared with the co-operative stage, but the differences were only statistically significant for the purchasing function. In this case there is a very high level of sufficiency of contact for interdependent KAM (nearly 90 per cent), but only about 60 per cent for co-operative KAM, with no real difference in perception according to seller and buyer. Perhaps at lower levels of KAM the relationship simply does not have enough importance to allow some buyers to devote much time to it.

Summary

There was a substantial difference between co-operative and interdependent relationships in the amount of customer contact afforded to selling companies (as judged by whether respondents considered it to be sufficient). Co-operative relationships tend to be left out in the cold more: only two-thirds gained enough access to even their main contact, compared with nearly 90 per cent of interdependent relationships.

Judged by its position as the function offering least sufficiency of access to suppliers, R&D is still a relatively remote process. Therefore co-development with suppliers is presumably still not very common.

4.6 EXCHANGE OF INFORMATION

How much information is shared?

Respondents were asked to what extent they exchanged information with their customer or supplier on a number of different subjects listed in Figure 4.6.

Question 6 *To what extent is there a two-way exchange of information with this supplier/buyer?* (Answered on Likert 5-point scale)

Stock availability

Product/service specification

Sales (total and mutual)

Product/service development

Costs

Marketing research

Business plans and strategies

FIGURE 4.6

Subjects for information exchange

The results can be summarised by scoring and totalling their answers, as shown in Table 4.13. The largest number of relationships, about half, fell into the middle category, equating to a level of exchange which was 'selective' on average. About a third had reached a level which was 'extensive'.

Scoring of overall extent of exchange of information	Total relationships
Base:	80
Very rarely (7–10)	2
	3%
Occasionally (11–17)	11
	12%
Selectively (18–24)	37
	46%
Extensively (25–31)	27
	34%
Freely (32–35)	3
	4%

See Appendix B for means of calculating score.

TABLE 4.13

Overall extent of two-way exchange of information

Good access to the buying company is likely to go hand in hand with high levels of information exchange and vice versa, so that the minority of relationships where participants were left out in the cold as far as contact is concerned are probably the same relationships which had not achieved a level beyond 'occasionally' in terms of information exchange. Indeed, this relationship was proved to a 1 per cent level of confidence (chi-squared value 32.729). High levels of contact mean more information exchange: 'out in the cold' means 'out of touch' as well.

Figure 4.7 appears to show that there is a difference between co-operative KAM relationships and interdependent KAM relationships in the amount of information exchanged; however, this result is only significant at a 10 per cent level of confidence, and must be treated with some caution. Nevertheless, the differences are consistent (*see* Table 4.14 below) and it does make logical sense, given the direct correlation between high levels of contact with information exchange, that if interdependent relationships have higher levels of contact, they should also have more information exchange than co-operative relationships. Although not shown, the chart of exchange of information by KAM success score was very similar.

'Out in the cold' means 'out of touch' as well.

FIGURE 4.7

Overall score on exchange of information by KAM relationship stage

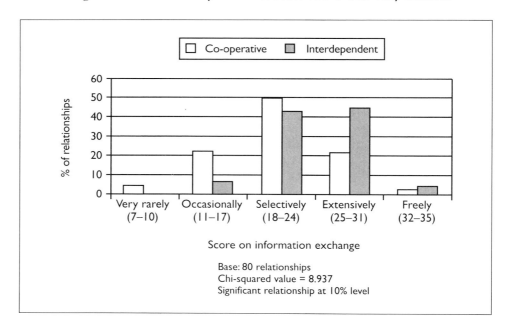

Base: 80 relationships
Chi-squared value = 8.937
Significant relationship at 10% level

What do people in key relationships talk about?

Table 4.14 shows both the percentage of respondents who said that information on each subject was either freely or extensively shared, as well as the overall score on information exchange. Exchange of information is a strong indicator of trust, particularly where it goes beyond the kind of information which is the minimum required to service the business.

Not surprisingly, the areas where information was most readily swapped were the basic ones of *stock availability*, *product/service specification* and *sales*. Information on *product/service development* was also exchanged quite freely in some relationships, a majority of which were at the interdependent stage. There is much less exchange on *costs*, *marketing research* and *business plans and strategies*. Presumably 'open-book' costing is still a rarity.

Subject of information exchange between selling co. and buying co.	Extent of information exchange	Total relationships	Co-operative KAM	Interdependent KAM
Base:		82	40	42
Stock availability	Freely/extensively	59%	48%	70%
	Score	3.70	3.44	3.95
Product/service specification	Freely/extensively	55%	41%	70%
	Score	3.71	3.44	3.98
Sales (total and mutual)	Freely/extensively	55%	45%	65%
	Score	3.59	3.38	3.79
Product/service development	Freely/extensively	48%	26%	73%
	Score	3.57	3.10	4.02
Costs	Freely/extensively	25%	20%	30%
	Score	2.83	2.74	2.90
Marketing research	Freely/extensively	23%	16%	30%
	Score	2.78	2.56	2.98
Business plans and strategies	Freely/extensively	18%	15%	21%
	Score	2.85	2.64	3.05

TABLE 4.14

Exchange of information between buying and selling companies by KAM relationship stage

Product/service specification: chi-squared value = 5.399; significant relationship at 2.5% level.

Product/service development: chi-squared value = 16.486; significant relationship at 0.5% level.

Scoring: 5 = freely; 3 = selectively; 1 = not at all.

The overall low levels of exchange on *marketing research* could have a number of causes:

- its results are considered as particularly sensitive;
- lack of willingness to share what they have paid money to gain;
- does not occur to them as relevant to pass on (buyers may even be unaware of information probably collected by the marketing department);
- simply not much research done.

Selling companies in interdependent relationships had much more access to information on product/service development.

In section 4.1 levels of occurrence of joint strategic planning were quite low and this distance at a strategic level is reflected again here, where sharing information on strategies and business plans was less than on any other subject investigated.

Across the board, companies with interdependent KAM relationships appeared to be sharing information more than those in co-operative KAM relationships, although the differences are only statistically proved for *product/service specification* and *product/service development*. Even on *stock availability*, it seems that companies were kept well informed in less than half of co-operative relationships. In contrast, about two-thirds of companies in interdependent KAM relationships were sharing this information freely or extensively.

Selling companies in interdependent relationships had much more access to information on *product/service development* than those in co-operative relationships. Relatively few of those at the lower level were really involved, i.e. only about one quarter, while three-quarters of those with interdependent KAM relationships appeared to be trusted with new product development information.

Summary

Information was most readily exchanged where necessary for basic management of transactions, i.e. on stock availability, product/service specification and sales.

Parties to interdependent relationships had a good deal more information than those in co-operative ones. It seems that being left 'out in the cold' in terms of contact with the buying company is accompanied by being left 'in the dark' as well. Co-operative relationships may work more on a strict 'need to know' basis than interdependent relationships.

The most marked difference was on product/service development, frequently a sensitive and secretive process. Selling companies with interdependent relationships were more often trusted to be told about, and perhaps even involved in, development than those with co-operative relationships.

Trust does not extend to sharing much about costs, marketing research or business plans, however. Restricting the flow of this kind of information seems to point to a persistent scepticism about the wisdom of giving suppliers sufficient access to allow them to build partnerships at a strategic level.

4.7 PRODUCT/SERVICE AND SUPPORT COMPLEXITY

Does complexity in the item sold make a difference to KAM relationships?

Overall, a little over half of these relationships involved a product/service which was perceived as very or quite complex. Very few suppliers agreed that the product/service they sold was simple (only in 4 out of 38 cases), while a quarter of buyers viewed what they bought as simple.

Nature of the product/service bought/supplied	Total relationships
Base:	80
Very complex	9
	11%
Quite complex	37
	46%
Neither complex nor simple	17
	21%
Quite simple	14
	18%
Very simple	3
	4%

TABLE 4.15
Complexity of product/service

It is logical to suggest that the intrinsic complexity of the product/service may have an effect on the closeness of the relationship, because of the dialogue and support requirements associated with complexity. Where the product requires a great deal of support, e.g. for technical reasons or because it is tailored to the customer's specifications, its sale will demand more communication and contact than a straightforward 'box-shifting' sale. That contact is an opportunity, perhaps an obligation, to develop closer KAM relationships. In fact, some producers of simple items deliberately complicate their offer with extra services and differentiators, mainly in order to avoid commodity status, but also to feed the customer relationship.

A quarter of buyers viewed what they bought as simple.

Figure 4.8 agrees with this logic, showing that complex products/services were more often associated with interdependent relationships than co-operative relationships, and products not considered as complex were more often associated with co-operative relationships than interdependent ones. However, the differences are not especially marked, and about 40 per cent of co-operative relationships in the survey involved products seen as complex.

FIGURE 4.8

Product/service complexity by KAM relationship stage

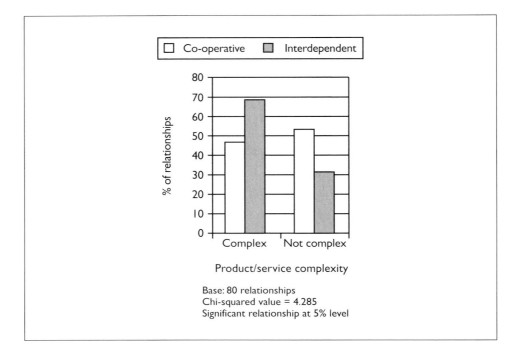

Base: 80 relationships
Chi-squared value = 4.285
Significant relationship at 5% level

Do levels of support affect KAM relationships?

Following this line of enquiry, support requirements were examined at three stages with the results shown in Table 4.16:

- selling and pre-introduction;
- introduction/installation;
- throughout lifetime of use/resale.

TABLE 4.16

Level of demand for support by KAM relationship stage

Timing	Level of demand for support	Co-operative	Interdependent
Base:	87	45	42
Selling and pre-introduction	Very/quite high	31 69%	29 69%
	Very/quite low	9 20%	7 17%
At introduction/installation	Very/quite high	23 51%	30 71%
	Very/quite low	17 38%	8 19%
Throughout lifetime of use/resale	Very/quite high	18 40%	24 57%
	Very/quite low	16 36%	10 24%

There are shifts in support demand as the sale progresses which appear to differ between the two stages of relationship, although this progression is not statistically proved here for each individual step. Table 4.16 shows that, in both cases, support needs are high during sell-in and pre-introduction, but whereas the level drops as the sale progresses through to introduction and later in relationships which have not progressed beyond the co-operative stage, it remains high in interdependent relationships through introduction, and even throughout the lifetime of the product/service.

These responses were also given a score to aggregate the overall support needs, and analysed by relationship stage in Figure 4.9.

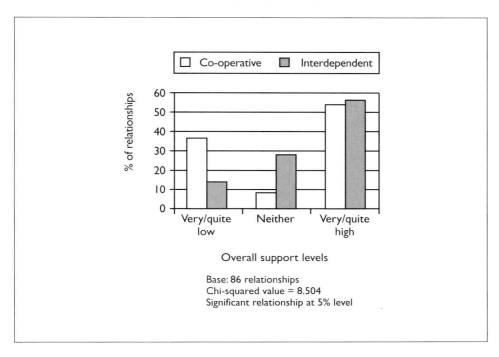

FIGURE 4.9

Overall level of demand for support by KAM relationship stage

Although low support products were most often handled in a co-operative relationship, high support products were just as often handled by a co-operative relationship as by an interdependent one.

The figure shows that relatively more co-operative relationships handled products/services with low support demands than did interdependent ones, which appears at first glance to agree with the premise that higher levels of support requirements would lead to closer KAM relationships and vice versa. Indeed, nearly three-quarters of products/services in the survey with low support requirements were sold in co-operative relationships.

However, at the other end of the scale, the situation is less clear. There were equal proportions of both stages of KAM relationship handling products/services with high support requirements, and these products/services were equally divided between the two relationship stages. So, although low support products were most often handled in a co-operative relationship, high support products were just as often handled by a co-operative relationship as by an interdependent one. The cause and effect linkage is not clear and/or simple, and is worthy of further investigation.

Summary

More buyers were inclined to see products/services as simple than were selling companies, which may be a further symptom of delusion on the part of the selling company. If they fail to appreciate the buyer's point of view, they are more likely to act inappropriately.

For example, if the buyer perceives a simple product/service as satisfying a simple need, with no advantage to be gained from getting more involved, it may be a waste of effort for the selling company to attempt to move the relationship from the co-operative to the interdependent stage.

While support levels required at the time of sell-in were similar in both types of relationship, support needs thereafter tended to drop off in co-operative relationships. The survey could not ascertain whether continuing high levels of support favour interdependent relationships, or whether cause and effect are reversed, in that selling companies are using ongoing support as a way of achieving closer relationships.

4.8 ADAPTATION TO CUSTOMER SPECIFICATION

How much do suppliers adapt for key buyers?

Adaptation, i.e. changing products or processes from the company standard, almost always involves cost to the supplier and therefore represents a serious commitment to the customer's business. This section examines the extent of adaptation and different elements of which it may be composed (*see* Figure 4.10).

Question 12 *To what extent have different aspects of your/your supplier's standard offer been adapted to meet your customer's/your specific needs?* (Answered on Likert 5-point scale)

Core product/service
Extra non-core services
Logistics
Information supply
Billing and paperwork
Marketing
Payment/finance

FIGURE 4.10

Aspects of adaptation of the selling company's offer

Table 4.17 and Figure 4.11 show adaptation of the selling company offer where it has been modified 'largely', 'quite a lot' or 'significantly'. The individual elements are listed in descending order of adaptation. They fall into two distinct groups: in the first group, *extra non-core services*, *core product/service*, *information supply* and *logistics*, there is considerably more modification than in the second group, *billing and paperwork*, *marketing* and *payment/finance*. In this first group of elements half of selling companies had made significant or greater changes to their standard offer.

Element of offer	Total	Degree of adaptation: largely, quite a lot or significantly Relationship success	
		Quite poor, neither poor nor good	Very or quite good
Base:	89	43	46
Extra non-core services	49%	33%	67%
Core product/service	49%	37%	63%
Information supply	49%	36%	61%
Logistics	49%	41%	59%
Billing and paperwork	36%	34%	37%
Marketing	32%	22%	28%
Payment/finance	25%	22%	28%
Average	41%	32%	49%

TABLE 4.17

Adaptation of selling company offer to buying company requirements by KAM relationship success

	Chi-squared values	Level of confidence
Extra non-core services	11.660	0.5%
Core product/service	5.934	2.5%
Information supply	4.919	2.5%
Marketing	4.175	5%

Scoring: 5 = largely; 3 = significantly; 1 = not at all.

It appears that selling companies are more prepared to modify any element other than *payment/finance*, which is understandable. At the same time, the accusation of inflexibility of payment terms is often levelled at selling companies. More creative terms seem to offer potential opportunities for gaining advantage over competitors, always provided that appropriate returns can still be secured.

FIGURE 4.11

Adaptation of selling company offer to buying company requirements by KAM relationship success

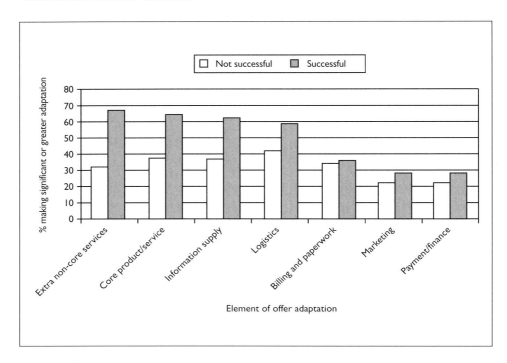

The conclusion that adaptation to customer needs leads to perceived success seems inescapable.

Is adapting to customer needs linked to success?

The responses were analysed by perceived relationship success. Figure 4.11 shows the same information as Table 4.17 more graphically. It is very clear that there is a link between adaptation to the customer's requirements and perception of success. In fact, it is in the first group of elements, *extra non-core services*, *core product/service*, *information supply* and *logistics*, that adaptation mainly occurs, and also where the real differences between the successful and less successful relationships are found.

Two-thirds of successful relationships had made significant or better changes to *extra non-core services*, compared with only one-third of the less successful relationships. There were also similarly marked differences in the modification made in *core products/services* and *information supply*, and also to *logistics* to a lesser extent. Although this survey cannot prove cause and effect, the conclusion that adaptation to customer needs leads to perceived success seems inescapable.

Although the analysis is not shown here, interdependent relationships seemed particularly to involve higher levels of adaptation of *extra non-core services* than do co-operative relationships. In fact, the higher level of adaptation of the standard offer of *extra non-core services* included in interdependent relationships is a key difference compared with co-operative relationships.

There could be a number of reasons for this emphasis on extra services in successful and interdependent relationships:

- customers in closer relationships may be better at leveraging the position of mutual commitment to gain additional benefits from selling companies, adding to their perception of the success of the relationship;

- selling companies may feel that offering such services cements their position with the customer and acts as a barrier to entry to competitors.

Summary

Adaptation of the selling company's offer was consistently greater in successful relationships than in less successful ones. Elements fell into two groups: 'extra non-core services', 'core product/service', 'information supply' and 'logistics'; and 'billing and paperwork', 'marketing' and 'payment/finance'. Adaptation was clearly greater in the first group than the second.

The greatest differences were in 'extra non-core services', 'core product/service', 'information supply' and 'logistics', where selling companies in successful relationships offered a good deal more than those in less successful ones. As a source of potentially substantial cost, however, the situation should be carefully monitored.

4.9 ALLOCATING COSTS AND MEASURING PERFORMANCE

How far does performance measurement go?

Selling companies were asked: 'To what extent do you quantify and allocate costs of all the support services this customer receives?', while buying companies were asked an equivalent question: 'Do you have systems which measure this supplier's performance regularly and quantitatively?'

Table 4.18 shows that in half of relationships cost allocation or performance measurement was handled 'completely'/'rigorously' or 'largely' in a way which would allow satisfactory assessment. The other half included a substantial proportion, about one in five of all relationships, in which cost allocation or performance measurement was 'not really' or 'not at all' conducted so that assessment of them could not be accurate.

Given the importance of these relationships, more comprehensive application of good systems of evaluation might have been expected. However, a variety of sources (e.g. McDonald, unpublished, 1997) suggest that many selling companies, for example, have relied on the traditional but simplistic gross margin as a performance measurement for customers and are only just beginning to recognise the need for a broader and more thorough evaluation.

TABLE 4.18

Degree of cost allocation/performance assessment

Extent of cost allocation/performance assessment	Total relationships
Base:	88
Completely/rigorously	17
	19%
Largely	28
	32%
Partly	27
	31%
Not really	14
	16%
Not at all	2
	2%

Given the importance of these relationships, more comprehensive application of good systems of evaluation might have been expected.

There were no significant differences according to whether the relationship was being measured by the buying side or the selling side, but Figure 4.12 shows the same answers broken down by stage of KAM relationship. It seems to suggest that a higher proportion of co-operative relationships are measured carefully than among interdependent relationships, but this result is only significant at a 10 per cent level, and so should be treated with some caution. It could be because companies in interdependent relationships can trust each other more and perhaps relax their surveillance to some extent. However, it could also be that the more sophisticated, interdependent relationships are just too difficult to cost properly because of the extent to which they have secured a wide variety of 'extra non-core services'.

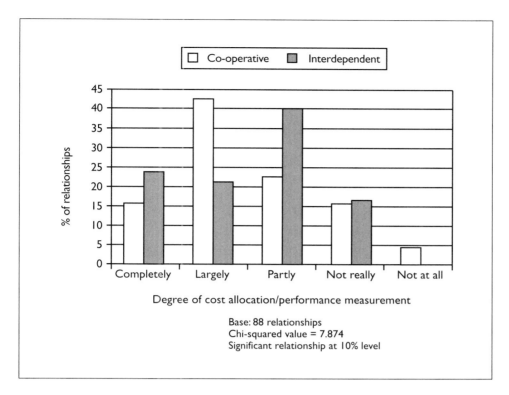

FIGURE 4.12

Degree of cost allocation/performance assessment by KAM relationship

At both levels there are a few not effectively measured at all, possibly more a reflection of a lack of competence in the respondent's company than super levels of trust. Results were also analysed by perceived success of the KAM relationship, but no significant linkage was found.

Summary

Only half of these key relationships were measured at all thoroughly. Interdependent relationships seemed to be subjected to lower levels of measurement than co-operative ones, possibly because of the greater occurrence of 'extra non-core services' which are difficult to monitor and measure.

4.10 CUSTOMER PROFITABILITY

Are gross margins on key customers' business better or worse than average?

Selling companies only were asked a number of questions about customer profitability which were obviously not appropriate to buying companies. A number of respondents did not reply, either because they did not have the information or could not readily access it, or because they considered it confidential. The results reported below are therefore based on rather small numbers.

Table 4.19 shows the gross margins earned on the business of key customers compared with the company average. In about a quarter of cases for which responses were given, the selling company had achieved a price allowing a higher than average gross margin. However, this success was counterbalanced by 40 per cent of the relationships in which the buying company had only achieved a price yielding a below-average gross margin.

TABLE 4.19

Gross margins compared with company average

Gross margin achieved v. company average	Total relationships
Base:	35
Higher	9
	26%
Same	12
	34%
Lower	14
	40%

How much gross margin is spent in extra 'cost to serve'?

These results illustrate the double-headed problem facing selling companies. First of all, many large buying companies are very successful at driving the price down anyway. Then they negotiate for, and/or receive, further added value, attention, information and services which add cost and cut into net contribution to the selling company's overheads, as demonstrated by Table 4.20.

% of sales	(i) Gross margin % of relationships	(ii) Contribution % of relationships
Base:	29	21
0–9%	5 17%	12 57%
10–19%	5 17%	8 38%
20–29%	8 28%	1 5%
30–39%	5 17%	0 0%
40%+	6 21%	0 0%

TABLE 4.20

Gross margins and residual contribution after deduction of attributable support costs

The range of gross margins (GM) earned was wide and spread fairly evenly between the deciles, with 20–29 per cent being the most common (*see* Figure 4.13). While some selling companies earned over 40 per cent GM, others start with what some would consider extremely low margins anyway, of less than 10 per cent. They have presumably evolved practices and processes which nevertheless allow them to be profitable at these low margins, but they could be perilously close to making a loss if their low margins were eroded even further.

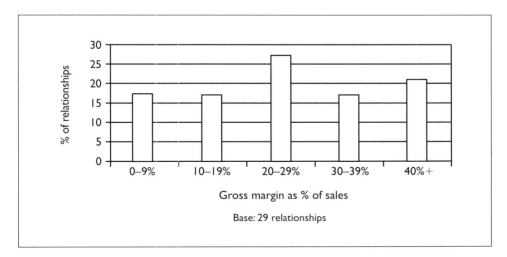

FIGURE 4.13

Distribution of gross margins earned from largest accounts

Table 4.20 also shows the percentage contribution remaining after costs attributable to each customer had been deducted. After deduction of these costs, no one reported having 40 per cent contribution or even as much as 30 per cent remaining and, indeed, only one relationship had more than 20 per cent left. A majority of these key accounts yielded less than 10 per cent contribution to overheads. Figure 4.14 shows this attrition of earnings more graphically.

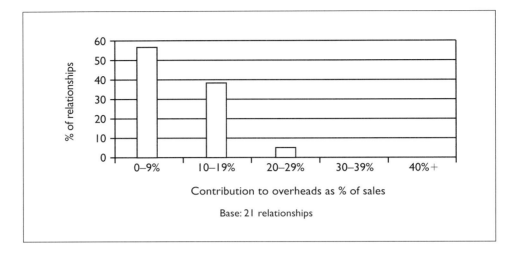

Base: 21 relationships

Overall, about two-thirds or more of the gross margin of these key accounts was eaten up by costs which respondents attributed to the account (calculated using the mid-point of the decile). Some key accounts absorbed over 80 per cent of the gross margin theoretically available. Given that these relationships are the biggest the supplier has, this loss of net income must represent a real cause for concern to selling companies. These findings confirm other studies (Wilson, 1997) which have shown that the largest customers quite often yield low contributions or are even loss-making.

Summary

Companies are often reluctant to disclose hard financial data, and therefore the base for this section was small. However, the results support findings from other studies, that selling companies' largest accounts often make very low, or even negative, contributions to overheads after deduction of all costs that should be attributed to them.

Two-thirds or more of the gross margin of these key accounts was eaten up by costs which respondents attributed to the account.

The problem starts when buying companies use their power to negotiate lower than average prices anyway, which a substantial minority had achieved. In some cases, however, selling companies had managed to gain higher than average prices, probably in order to cover additional services.

4.11 SHARE OF PURCHASES

How much business have sellers secured?

Earlier, in section 4.2, the question of whether investment in the relationships would lead to greater success was considered. Here the question of whether investment in the relationships appears at least to be linked to a greater volume of business is examined, based on the business available from each customer.

Respondents were asked what share of their/the customer's purchases of this type of product the selling company had secured (*see* Table 4.21). In previous work, the different levels of KAM relationship were linked with supplier status as follows:

- 'basic' = one of several/many;

- 'co-operative' = preferred supplier;

- 'interdependent' and 'integrated' = sole supplier.

Share of products/services bought of this type	Total relationships
Base:	86
Under 10%	13
	15%
10–24%	7
	8%
25–49%	14
	16%
50–75%	18
	21%
Over 75%	34
	40%

TABLE 4.21

Share of purchases of same product/service type

About 40 per cent of relationships had gained half or less of their customer's purchases in this product category. However, it is not possible to judge from this information whether they had the products to fulfil the opportunity, or whether there is some other reason why reaching sole supplier status is not viable. In one case, for example, purchases had to alternate between one brand and another to avoid problems of disease resistance, so maximum sales were realistically 50 per cent of the buying company's spend.

Do closer relationships secure greater share of spend?

A key question for suppliers is whether, if they invest in the relationship, they are likely to gain a higher share of the customer's business. Analysis of share of purchases by stage of relationship reveals a significant linkage between the two, though not which comes first, the business then the closer relationship, or the relationship leading to winning more business. The difference between interdependent relationships and co-operative ones is illustrated in Figure 4.15.

Figure 4.15

Share of purchases of this product/service type by KAM relationship score

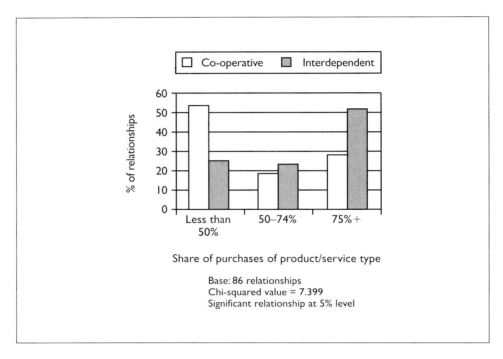

Share of purchases of product/service type

Base: 86 relationships
Chi-squared value = 7.399
Significant relationship at 5% level

Half of interdependent relationships had gained over 75 per cent of the buying company's relevant purchases, compared with only a quarter of co-operative relationships. At the opposite end of the scale, the reverse was found: half of co-operative relationships had gained less than 50 per cent of the customer's business, compared with a quarter of interdependent ones.

That the split is not completely clear-cut is not surprising. There will be cases where multiple sourcing does not suit the buyer, particularly on products/services which are low volume, low strategic importance and low in opportunity for savings. They may not be worth the amount of attention and management that multiple sourcing would require. There are also many reasons why, however good the relationship, the supplier may not be able to cover a substantial amount of the buying company's purchases of the category, e.g. for geographical or technical reasons.

Half of interdependent relationships had gained over 75 per cent of the buying company's purchases, compared with only a quarter of co-operative relationships.

Summary

Closer, more sophisticated relationships are linked with securing a greater share of the customer's business.

Half of the selling companies with relationships at the interdependent stage had secured over three-quarters of their customers' purchases of similar goods or services, and this was double the proportion of co-operative relationships.

4.12 MARKET SITUATION

What does the external environment look like?

Respondents were asked a number of questions relating to the market(s) in which they operate. In theory, factors such as competitive intensity and uncertainty should affect the stage of development of relationships. It could be assumed that interdependent ones, which have an advantage over other suppliers and have more contact and more information exchange, will be less at risk than more distant, co-operative relationships.

A rating on overall uncertainty was sought directly, and also a rating of factors which tend to contribute to market turbulence, i.e. rate of market growth, rate of innovation and competitive intensity. The last were combined to give a score on market turbulence. Table 4.22 shows respondents' views of their market situation in both terms.

Factor	Rating	Total companies
Base:		36
Uncertainty in core markets	Very or quite high	17 47%
	Neither high nor low/very or quite low	19 53%
Market turbulence in core markets	Very or quite high	19 53%
	Neither high nor low/very or quite low	17 47%

TABLE 4.22

Uncertainty and market turbulence in core markets

*However analysed,
there were no
significant
differences apparent
in relationship
development
according to
market factors.*

Companies were equally divided between those who felt that uncertainty or turbulence in their market situation was 'very' or 'quite high', and those who felt theirs was either 'low' or 'neither high nor low'. There was a close correlation between the two kinds of rating.

Because buying companies were reporting on their company's market situation rather than the supply side market, it is generally inappropriate to analyse together buying and selling company views on further points about market circumstances.

How does the market environment affect relationships?

In fact, however analysed, there were no significant differences apparent in relationship development according to market factors: neither by measure of uncertainty/turbulence in the market, nor by the individual elements which made up the derived measure of market turbulence, i.e. competitive intensity, market growth or rate of innovation. Nor were there any significant differences apparent by role in the survey (i.e. buying v. selling).

This lack of differentiation may occur for several reasons:

• market situation really has no effect on buyer/supplier relationship development;

• the effects of market situation, however assessed, are too complex and varied to be investigated in this way;

• market situation should be assessed by different means.

Intuitively, the first possibility seems wrong, although it may be that these relationships 'take on a life of their own' and develop more by instinct and personal goodwill than by logical response to the company's market needs.

Certainly the second possibility seems to apply. For example, it could make sense to invest in relationship building where market circumstances are threatening, but not necessarily just because the market is turbulent, when it may make sense to keep options open. If market circumstances are threatening, they may have a potential negative impact on seller and buyer alike which would drive the two towards a closer alliance. On the other hand, buyer power could be a part of the threat to suppliers, and customers might use that power to shop around rather than enter close partnerships.

The third possibility is also relevant. Given the range of reactions possible, market situation probably needs analysis in greater detail in order to be amenable to proper interpretation. In addition, market situation alone may be insufficient anyway as a predictor of behaviour without an understanding of how each company perceives and reacts to different circumstances. For example, company culture and attitude to risk will influence their reading of, and reaction to, any market situation.

In fact, it is very difficult to assess the effect of the market on relationship development through this kind of research – there is such a wide range and variety of market influences that could be relevant. These influences produce a range of strategies among sellers and buyers which may, or may not, be compatible with each other in terms of relationship development. The next stage of qualitative research should probe this area to establish which of the above three applies, or indeed whether all three do.

Do margin levels affect KAM relationships?

Respondents were also asked about average margins in their core markets, again in order to examine whether they had an effect on relationship development. Table 4.23 shows the results of that question, and also a summary question on how the company viewed the overall prospects in its core markets.

Factor	Rating	Total companies
Base:		35
Average margins in core markets	Very or quite high	7 20%
	Neither high nor low	11 31%
	Very or quite low	16 46%
Overall outlook in core markets	Excellent or good	31 89%
	Neither good nor poor	4 11%
	Poor	0 0%

TABLE 4.23
Average margins and overall outlook

The table shows that only a fifth of respondents felt that their margins were at all high, a third were neutral and about half thought they were either very or quite low. There were no discernible differences according to stage of relationship development. Differences by role in the survey were also not significant, although buyers were possibly slightly more positive than selling companies.

Respondents were almost all positive about the outlook overall. However, since half had reported a high degree of uncertainty in their core markets and half had also reported low margins, this appears to be an outbreak of rather unwarranted optimism. It suggests a certain 'it will be alright on the night' approach, a kind of corporate delusion or failure to reflect accurately unpopular reality, which can be very dangerous to companies.

Summary

The survey was unable to detect any comprehensible differences in relationship development caused by market factors.

Since it seems highly unlikely that market influences have no impact on key relationships, it is more likely that the interactions between the markets, the companies and their trading partners are too complex to be investigated by this kind of survey.

Approaching half of the companies in the survey felt their margins were low to some degree. In spite of this and other negative factors, a large majority felt optimistic abut their prospects.

About half thought their margins were either very or quite low.

5

Discussion

5.1 THE KAM ENVIRONMENT

The location of Key Account Management within the buying/selling dyad

Key Account Management is a complex subject. On the one side, it represents the interface between the company and its most important points of contact with the external world. At the same time, in order to deliver its promises to customers, KAM has to link in with the company's internal processes and culture. KAM is, very much, where the 'inside' meets the 'outside'.

The scope of this study can be described in terms of Figure 5.1. Key Account Management (not necessarily the key account manager) is placed at the centre of the trading partnership. It interfaces with both companies' processes and their products/services, which are in turn influenced by the external and internal environments. Survey questions focused on the key relationships themselves, their interface with aspects of the product/service concerned and processes, plus certain demographics to check the spread of companies involved. The internal environment was considered too complex for inclusion in this kind of survey, but an attempt was made to examine the effect of the external environment as it is translated into an impact on KAM. However, this also proved too complex and it was not possible to draw any useful conclusions from the data collected.

KAM is ... where the 'inside' meets the 'outside'.

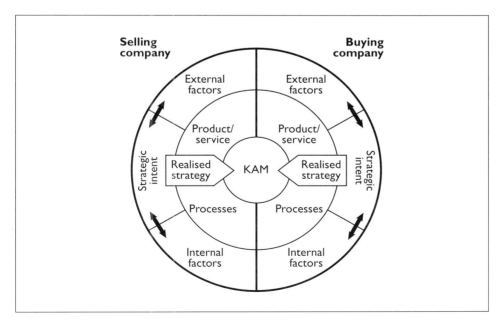

FIGURE 5.1

Key Account Management within the environment of buying and selling companies

Business with key customers and suppliers will be affected by the external environment, regardless of the fact that this study could not throw new light on the mechanisms of its impact. Overall economics, development of technology, politics and competition are all likely to be important. The external environment may be translated into an impact on the KAM relationship through the medium of the product and all its attendant aspects, though not only by this means.

Similarly, the internal environment will play a large part in the organisation's capabilities and willingness to apply them within the key relationship. The culture, especially in respect of attitudes towards customers and key account managers, will affect delivery of the offer made, as will systems, staff and other elements. They will tend to take effect through the medium of processes, but again, not exclusively.

This model indicates the range and complexity of the Key Account Manager's job and suggests that a substantial part of it should be directed internally.

Both the internal and external environment should be analysed in the development of the company's strategic intent. Ultimately, it will be the actualisation of whatever strategies the company has specified which will influence the KAM relationship, on routes to market, product development or pricing, for example.

The role of key account managers

Obviously, the requirement of the key account manager's role stems from the position of key account management within the buyer/seller dyad shown in Figure 5.1. Although the immediate concerns of the Key Account Manager will be with the products/services the customer has bought or might be persuaded to buy and the processes through which they are delivered, the model shows that he or she will need to know how to operate within the strategy and surrounding environment as well.

The key account manager role has previously been viewed as an outward, customer-facing position which would no doubt require him or her to be out of the office a good deal of the time. However, this model indicates the range and complexity of the key account manager's job and suggests that a substantial part of it should be directed internally. The role is increasingly seen as one of general management, co-ordination and development, working through colleagues who may spend more time with customer staff than the key account manager, though with no less of a customer focus.

The situation within the buying company has a parallel structure and complementary position: the supply chain manager. However, that does not necessarily mean that suppliers are handled by buyers in a manner which is entirely reciprocal to the way that suppliers handle buyers. Indeed, this and other studies have demonstrated a number of differences in approach by the two sides. Buying companies tend to treat their relationships with selling companies and their representatives with greater reserve and less commitment. They are also less likely to be as selective in the number of suppliers they will treat as key to their business, which will limit the importance and focus on each.

Previous work (McDonald, Millman and Rogers, 1996) discussed the demands on the person at the heart of this microcosm, on the selling company side, from the points of view of both the selling company and the buying company. Each side had different requirements and expectations which were potentially in conflict. Given the range and positioning of the role shown in this model, this finding is hardly surprising.

5.2 RELATIONSHIP DIAGNOSTIC INDICATORS

KAM relationship development model

Figure 5.2 shows the stages of KAM relationships in order of increasing sophistication. The model is depicted as a pyramid, partly because it appears that the number of each type of relationship decreases as the level of sophistication and closeness increases, and partly because it implies that each stage depends on the continued fulfilment of the requirements of the previous stage. Parallels may also be drawn with Maslow's hierarchy of needs (*see* later this section).

The incidence of each type of relationship was not comprehensively determined by this study, although a scheme was developed which would enable such research to be carried out quite simply. The study does give some indications of relative proportions, however. At first sight the survey seemed to have found equal numbers of co-operative and interdependent relationships, but on further examination this was shown not to be the case (*see* section 5.4): co-operative relationships were more common than interdependent ones.

Only one integrated relationship was found, suggesting that they are the least common. This would make sense, since they are very close and absorbing relationships, and companies would find it difficult to manage more than a very few at most. The incidence of basic relationships would need more investigation, as this survey effectively rules out their inclusion through its focus on the largest three accounts. However, discussion with companies often puts most of their customer relationships, even key relationships, in this class. Overall, this yields the order of relationships shown in Figure 5.2 in terms of numbers as well as stage of development.

FIGURE 5.2

Development of relationships between buying and selling companies

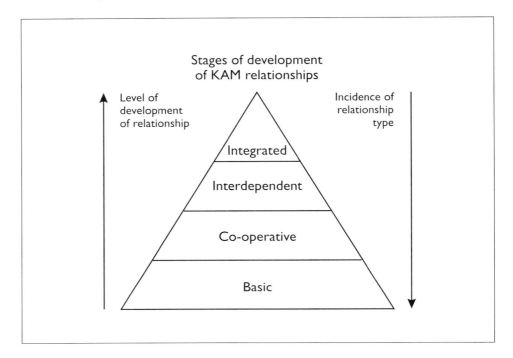

Stages of development
of KAM relationships

Level of
development
of relationship

Incidence of
relationship
type

Integrated

Interdependent

Co-operative

Basic

Characteristics of KAM relationships

This research tested a set of statements about the relationship between selling companies and their key accounts which represents a simple diagnostic scheme for quickly determining the stage of development of the relationship. Stages were calibrated against a theoretical model of what ideal responses would be at each stage (*see* Appendix B), and included a band of scores on either side of the theoretical score.

The scheme was tested by the behaviour of the different relationship groups against logic and the observations of other authors. Results stood up well in describing associated characteristics of the relationship and the ways in which they would be expected to be linked with the stage of relationship development. However, it was only possible to test two of the relationship stages, co-operative and interdependent, because the methodology of this project tended to eliminate exploratory and basic KAM, and because integrated KAM is a rarity (only one such case was found here, and most authorities only cite a few incidences).

The scheme should continue to be tested in further research, particularly where KAM relationships can be observed in greater detail alongside the diagnostic test, in order to confirm that it does indeed have wide validity.

Summarising the diagnostic indicators applied, it seems that cessation of competitor monitoring by the buying company is unlikely to occur in either relationship stage. Trust may develop within the relationship, but apparently not blind trust to that extent. Buyers may feel that they must maintain a benchmark for their supplier's performance, perhaps to defend internally their commitment to the relationship, as well as making sure that they are still getting best value. Earlier research has shown that buyers consider that suppliers who withhold new opportunities to give added value are abusing their trust (Lohtia and Krapfel, 1994). Anyway, it seems that they are not prepared to risk leaving the matter to goodwill.

Internal adaptation in terms of setting up cross-functional teams, a spirit of partnership, social association and barriers to exit are commonly found within these relationships. Joint strategic planning is much less common, but is found more often in successful relationships. This kind of survey information does not suggest which comes first: whether relationships which become successful then start to plan together; whether planning and commitment make the relationship successful; or even whether it is the activity itself which improves perceptions of success.

While the underlying 'cause and effect' remains to be determined by other means, the connection between joint strategic planning and success of itself suggests that companies trying to make progress within a relationship might use this approach, even if it were not logically self-evident that planning has to be better than not planning. Planning together is also likely to be a good deal more meaningful than a plan devised by one side or the other in isolation. Having said that, recent interviews with buying companies have revealed that many selling companies are doing just that: many suppliers deliver a pre-prepared 'strategic plan' without involving buyers in its development, and consequently fail to get their support. Such plans are seen as no more than the standard start-of-year presentation of targets for supplier's sales, without regard to buyer's needs, and are not considered positively.

Buyers consider that suppliers who withhold new opportunities to give added value are abusing their trust. Anyway ... they are not prepared to risk leaving the matter to goodwill.

Joint strategic planning is much less common, but is found more often in successful relationships.

Many suppliers deliver a pre-prepared 'strategic plan' without involving buyers in its development, and consequently fail to get their support. Such plans are seen as no more than the standard start-of-year presentation ... and are not considered positively.

Hierarchy of need satisfaction

To some extent, KAM relationships can be viewed as a mirror of the hierarchy of an individual's needs originally defined by Maslow (Maslow, 1943). In Maslow's hierarchy, basic needs have to be satisfied before individuals can develop to higher levels of expression of their existence, with different needs. People who are starving or dying of disease concern themselves first with dealing with their condition before they look for security or friendship. In other words, physiological needs, e.g. for food and health, must be satisfied before an individual can become interested in higher levels of need, such as society and status.

Maslow distinguished seven innate needs (Buchanan and Huczynski, 1985):

1. Physiological

2. Safety

3. Love

4. Esteem

5. Self-actualisation

6. Freedom of enquiry and expression

7. Need to know and to understand.

The development of KAM relationships can be seen in the same way, where the needs of both parties replace the needs of the individual (*see* Figure 5.3). At its most basic, the relationship satisfies needs to receive goods and money at a strictly transactional level. If these needs are met, the relationship might go on to meet others, such as the desire for a continuous stream of income or a reliable source of supply. At its most sophisticated, the relationship could play a part in reaching the strategic goals of both organisations.

In this model a basic KAM relationship satisfies 'physiological' needs such as efficient transactions, i.e. product/service delivery, while co-operative KAM adds satisfaction of 'safety' needs, perhaps reducing the risk of losing the business, but must continue to satisfy the 'physiological' needs as well. The parallel is useful because it emphasises the principle that each stage of the relationship must satisfy the needs of the previous stages before it can move on to satisfy 'higher' level needs. This prediction from Maslow's theory seems to match common experience of KAM: suppliers often have to prove themselves before buyers will invest the time to bring the relationship to a more strategic level.

Each stage of the relationship must satisfy the needs of the previous stages before it can move on to satisfy 'higher' level needs.

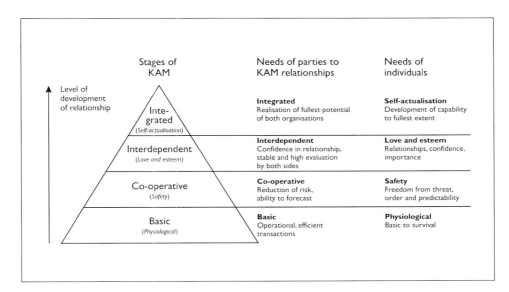

Figure 5.3
**Hierarchy of needs: individual
v. parties to KAM relationship**

Maslow also hypothesised that if the individual's lower level needs ceased to be met, then he or she would lose interest in higher level needs and revert to the unsatisfied state. If the analogy holds for KAM relationships on this point as well, a co-operative KAM relationship would be expected to revert to a basic relationship should it cease to satisfy 'safety' needs, if the supplier's deliveries became unreliable or they failed to support the buyer with emergency back-up, for example.

Alternatively, it could be that the KAM relationship takes a course not available to individuals, which is to split and separate. It would take further enquiry into disintegrating KAM relationships to establish which is more likely to occur.

5.3 RELATIONSHIP SUCCESS

Portfolio approach to relationship success and relationship development

The major question must be, 'If we put time, effort and money into developing relationships with our trading partners, will they be more successful commercially?' Given that business is about making money, financial success must be the overriding criterion by which KAM relationships are judged. Nevertheless, since the future cannot be foretold as a definite number, various other criteria become relevant in so far as they have a bearing on financial success.

There is indeed a link between KAM relationship stage and success, but ... this 'rule' does not always hold.

Analysis of relationship stage by success rating showed relationships distributed into the 'lower development stage/lower success' band plus those in the 'higher development stage/higher success' band in a ratio of 2 : 1, compared with the number in the 'lower development stage/higher success' band and the 'higher development stage/lower success' band. This result suggests that there is indeed a link between KAM relationship stage and success, but the existence of a substantial minority which do not conform means that this 'rule' does not always hold.

For example, there were some successful relationships found in the survey which are only co-operative. This is explained by McDonald and Rogers's business strength v. customer attractiveness matrix on strategies for relationship development (Figure 5.4: McDonald and Rogers, 1998). For alternative versions of this matrix, *see* Olsen and Ellram (1997).

Figure 5.4

KAM strategies by selling company business strength and buying company attractiveness

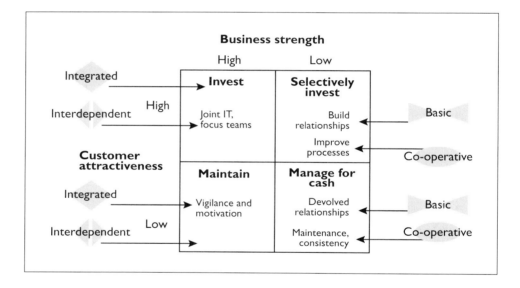

McDonald and Rogers's thesis is that lower level relationships can fall into two categories (*see* the right-hand side of the matrix). First, there are those where the customer is attractive and even if the selling company's current business strength is low (top right-hand box), they may decide to work at increasing it because investment in the relationship is judged to be worthwhile. Second, there are others where the customer is not attractive, and relationship development is not worthwhile (bottom right-hand box), but a well-managed transaction-focused relationship can be profitable, and may indeed be very important too, particularly in volume terms. However, if relationships are unattractive and also unprofitable, then there is clearly cause for concern and action.

A well-managed transaction-focused relationship can be profitable, and may indeed be very important.

Interdependent relationships will fall into the left-hand side of the matrix. If the relationship has reached the interdependent stage and is unsuccessful, then ways of changing it need to be examined. This conclusion is obvious enough, and it might be thought that any company with this view of a relationship must be actively engaged in resolving the problem. In fact, the information on customer profitability presented here and other research as well (Wilson, 1997) shows that there are too many of these situations around for them to be mere transitory hiccups. In fact, less successful relationships seem to have endured as long as more successful ones, and there were as many of the former that had lasted 15 years or more as there were of the latter. It is to be hoped that they have not been such poor performers throughout their extended lifetime.

Companies should be very clear about selecting the right relationships to develop in the first place, and then manage them extremely carefully.

Relationship profitability

Some of these relationships are probably perceived as unsuccessful because the company has not consciously conducted a full financial analysis and has not recognised the extent of the problem. Others represent long-term, intransigent situations into which companies have been cornered, perhaps by a determined buyer, optimistic key account manager, or poorly written contract, where they lack the courage to take the necessary action. Firmness can pay off handsomely: one loss-making company, admittedly with dominant shares in its core markets, implemented 'an aggressively upward pricing policy' with great success and a return to excellent profits within two years.

There does appear to be a link between relationship development stage and success, but given that a proportion of relationships can reach higher levels and still prove unsuccessful, companies should be very clear about selecting the right relationships to develop in the first place, and then manage them extremely carefully.

Financial satisfaction is obviously an important element in the composite success rating. Although respondents were happy with half of the relationships in financial terms, they were not happy with a third of them. This represents a very substantial minority, and it should be stressed again that these relationships are also the companies' biggest.

Financial satisfaction did not seem to depend on the level of development of the relationship (co-operative or interdependent) or role (supplier or buyer). Financial satisfaction would be presumed to be strongly bound up with the perception of success of the relationship, but a substantial minority (one-sixth) reported relationships that the respondent considered financially unsatisfactory as being seen as extremely successful and important by the CEO.

Most (selling companies) lost a large amount of the margin in servicing the customer.

Customer profitability, in terms of gross margins and deviation from company averages, is probably more easily measured than the equivalent from the buying company side, which would be suppliers' prices compared with competitors' and, where products are resold without further processing, differential margins available from reselling. The latter would involve constant research with competitors, and genuine benchmark prices are not easily achieved in business-to-business markets where list prices are generally meaningless for large buyers. Nevertheless, the survey did reveal that buyers do indeed attempt comparison by constantly checking the competition.

In fact, real customer profitability measures, taking into account all directly attributable costs such as technical advice, selling costs, dedicated R&D, socialising, etc., do not appear to be achieved much more often than total supplier value measures. Of those selling companies that did respond to this part of the survey, most lost a large amount of the margin in servicing the customer. There is already a good deal of evidence from a number of sources to support this result, from the selling company side, and in many cases the largest customers are actually loss-making.

5.4 SUPPLIER DELUSIONS

Positive interpretations of reality

Key account managers may or may not be different from traditional salespeople, but a predisposition to take a positive view of the relationship with the customer might have been anticipated anyway. For example, this survey shows that, overall, more suppliers considered their KAM relationships to be at a more advanced stage than did the buyers.

This raises the issue that much of the research on KAM has been conducted with key account managers, and relatively little with buyers or even with other people within the selling company. This survey included both suppliers and buyers to gain that balance, although they were not parties to the same relationships. Seeing a subject through the eyes of someone with a persistent bias in viewpoint, for whatever reason, results in a real danger of misinterpretation and misreading reality.

There are obviously at least two parties to a relationship. A relationship cannot be taken further than the less committed party chooses to go, because that would mean the other party will be advancing on its own, which is not a relationship. Therefore the correct evaluation of the stage of a relationship is the perception of the less committed party to it. This argument is shown diagrammatically in Figure 5.5.

A relationship cannot be taken further than the less committed party chooses to go.

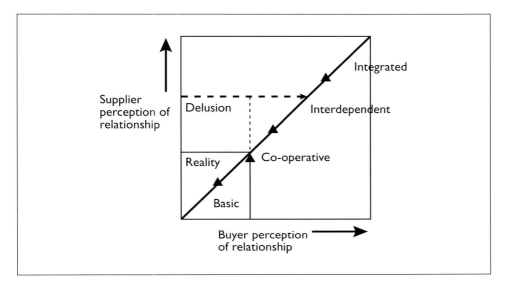

Figure 5.5

Stage of relationship according to supplier and buyer perspectives

The real extent of the relationship will always be represented by a square. If, however, either supplier or buyer perceptions are different from those of the other party, a rectangle results, which represents a mismatch between what one side believes and what the other accepts. In the example shown in Figure 5.5, the supplier believes that an interdependent relationship has been reached with the customer while the customer only sees the relationship as co-operative, and therefore in reality it cannot be more than co-operative.

Suppliers tend to overrate their relationships by a factor of two.

In this survey, two-thirds of relationships rated by suppliers appeared to have achieved the interdependent stage, while only one-third of relationships rated by buyers appeared to have reached the same level. This suggests that suppliers tend to overrate their relationships by a factor of two: they believe they have twice as many interdependent relationships as they probably have in reality. If this is so, then only about a third of relationships genuinely reached the interdependent level. Hence the conclusion that KAM research needs to spread its net wider than just key account managers in order to arrive at valid assessments.

5.5 CONTACT AND AWARENESS

Contact mapping

The survey examined the extent of contact between different functions of the buying company and the selling company taken as a whole and not split by function. As a way of visualising the pattern, lines of contact of different strength may be mapped onto Porter's value chain model of a company. In Figure 5.6, heavier lines denote more contact, in terms of the proportion considering that there was sufficient contact.

FIGURE 5.6

Contact between selling and buying companies by relationship stage

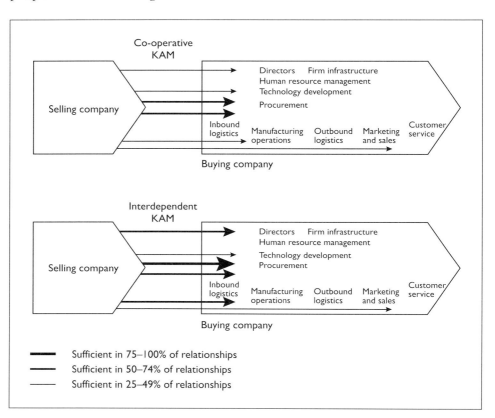

In co-operative relationships over 50 per cent of selling companies have sufficient contact only with the most immediate buying company functions, purchasing and inbound logistics.

Mapped in this way, the differences between the two relationship stages are highlighted. In interdependent relationships over 50 per cent of selling companies have sufficient contact with almost all buying company functions (except R&D); in contrast, in co-operative relationships over 50 per cent of selling companies have sufficient contact *only* with the most immediate buying company functions, purchasing and inbound logistics. The map illustrates the fact that in interdependent relationships there is a much heavier traffic between buyers and sellers than in co-operative relationships.

In both types of relationship, contact with R&D is still rather less than with other functions. It could perhaps be identified as a 'second-tier' function in terms of contact with suppliers. However, partners in interdependent relationships claimed high levels of freely or extensively exchanged information on product/service development, which could mean that information on buying company development is shared indirectly, and not through direct contact with R&D departments.

Original models showed the internal elements within each company as general 'operations' or 'clerks' etc. However, to establish the nature and degree of penetration of each organisation by the other, it would be useful to investigate further who actually interacts with whom as a route to better understanding of organisational permutations and possibilities. This representation of the contacts between trading partners as in Figure 5.6 could be amplified and developed as another way of depicting KAM relationship stages (*see* section 1.2).

Points of contact are identified as specific functions ... because the interaction will primarily be determined by 'why' and therefore 'which function'.

Figure 5.7 shows two representations of co-operative relationships. In the original model the various points of contact are identified as generalisations of the organisation structure, whereas in the proposed model they are identified as specific functions. This approach seems more useful, because the interaction will primarily be determined by 'why' and therefore 'which function' or specialism, rather than 'what level' of seniority.

In the proposed model inbound logistics (buying company) and order processing (selling company) are shown in the inner core of the relationship, alongside the purchasing manager and key account manager. The survey found a dual and fairly equal emphasis on contact with the purchasing manager and with the customer's inbound logistics in co-operative relationships. Indeed, a very strong rapport is often built up between the staff on both sides who manage day-to-day delivery. They are in frequent communication, often much more than the key account manager and purchasing manager, and they help each other out and solve a lot of problems together. (The survey did not clarify whether indeed it is that department or the key account manager with whom contact is normal, hence the question mark against the selling company's contact point.)

No changes are proposed to the diamond-shaped model of the interdependent relationship (*see* section 1.2), which already anticipates high levels of contact and therefore includes close interfaces.

FIGURE 5.7

Mid-KAM relationship model (McDonald, Millman and Rogers, 1994) v. proposed co-operative **KAM** model

Selling companies in co-operative relationships are left 'out in the cold' and 'in the dark' too.

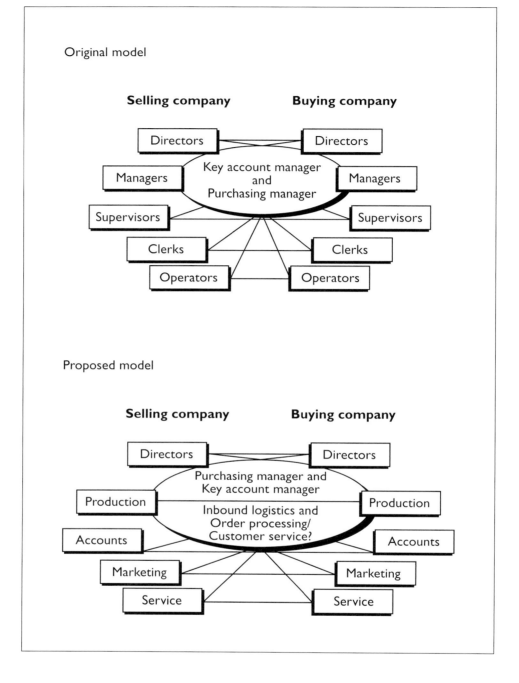

Access to information and awareness of change

It is a reasonable assumption that the greater the contact, the greater the amount of information which will be exchanged. The observation that selling companies in co-operative relationships are left 'out in the cold' and 'in the dark' too should therefore come as no surprise.

There is a parallel between the functions which interact at a satisfactory level and the kind of information which is exchanged: in co-operative relationships both the functions (purchasing and inbound logistics) and the information shared (stocks, sales and specifications) are those required as a minimum to deliver the offer at an operational level. After that the level drops off substantially for them, whereas in interdependent relationships the functional interaction and information shared are both greater in degree and in range.

In interdependent relationships the functional interaction and information shared are both greater in degree and in range.

This poses a problem for selling companies in co-operative relationships. Although this relationship level might otherwise be appropriate *to their knowledge*, how good is their knowledge likely to be? If circumstances change, are they likely to know, or know soon enough, to be able to respond appropriately and ahead of competitors who may already supply the customer as well?

In many cases selling companies that seem to have a perfectly adequate track record in meeting the customer's requirements lose the business to another company which may actually be weaker in that particular product range but have a close relationship with the customer in other areas. These competitors can put together a compelling and imaginative proposition, based on better customer awareness and understanding. On some occasions they are even assisted by some of the customer's staff who see advantage in developing the business with a supplier with whom they work very closely anyway. This pattern is well known to many selling companies caught up in supplier consolidation initiatives.

Competitors can put together a compelling and imaginative proposition, based on better customer awareness and understanding.

This suggests that sellers in co-operative relationships need to make strenuous efforts to gain information, because it may not just come to them otherwise. They should widen their range of sources as much as possible and react to any signs of change, at least by actively probing the nature of the change. In many companies customer intelligence information is patchily captured, poorly organised and barely interpreted. Excellence in handling the information they do have could go a long way to ameliorating the shortage.

Product/service development in interdependent relationships

One of the most marked differences found between co-operative and interdependent relationships was the amount of information exchanged on the subject of development: three-quarters of those in interdependent

Sellers in co-operative relationships need to make strenuous efforts to gain information.

If a new product is designed around a specific product, it will be very difficult for a different supplier with a different product specification to make a proposal to the buying company which is at all appropriate.

relationships were sharing information on the subject freely or extensively, compared with just one-quarter of those in co-operative relationships.

Access to development projects is a major opportunity for both parties. Selling companies can suggest solutions which are those they can supply at good margins or ones where they have a unique offer. If a new product is designed around a specific product, it will be very difficult for a different supplier with a different product specification to make a proposal to the buying company which is at all appropriate.

Although some buying companies are nervous about divulging their plans to suppliers, there can be major benefits for them as well. The buying company can take advantage of the supplier's latest R&D to make sure their own product is as far advanced and ahead of the market as possible. It can also be designed to deliver the optimum performance in the most cost-effective way. Figure 5.8 shows how the final cost of a new product is affected by the stage at which decisions on its design are made.

FIGURE 5.8

Cost impact of upstream action in product development (European Institute of Purchasing and Supply)

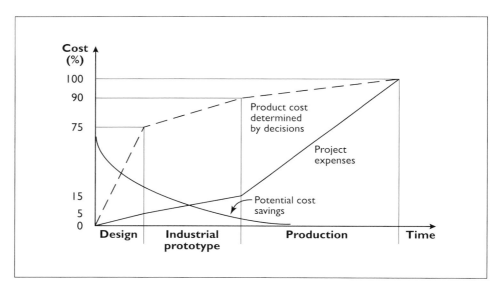

This graph shows the difference that the stage at which a design decision is taken makes to the final costs and expenses of a development project. The graph applies to development of a new industrial product, but would hold true to varying degrees for any similar project. It illustrates that the first stage, design, absorbs 5 per cent of the final project costs, but is responsible for determining 75 per cent of the ultimate product cost. The second stage, prototyping, adds another 10 per cent to the project cost, and fixes a further 15 per cent of the product cost. It is in the last phase, production, that 85 per cent of the project costs are spent, but by this time the product cost of sale is very nearly fixed, and only 10 per cent of it can be affected at this late stage.

In summary, a large share of the cost of sale is committed at a very early stage in development, and only marginal changes are possible later. Any potential to save cost falls off very quickly during and after the design period. Therefore including in the development process a supplier who is able and willing to contribute can be a major benefit to a buying company. However, as new products are often a critical part of a company's strategy to gain competitive advantage, such information can only be shared with trading partners who are well known and whose commitment is trusted, which is likely to be in more than a co-operative relationship.

Including in the development process a supplier who is able and willing to contribute can be a major benefit to a buying company.

5.6 STRATEGIC PLANNING

Existence of strategic planning processes

For partners to formulate joint strategic plans a number of other processes need to precede the planning process, which might then become a reiterative cycle (*see* Figure 5.9).

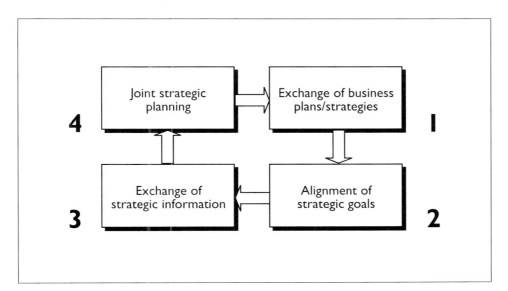

FIGURE 5.9

Strategic planning processes in KAM relationships

It seems logical to start with an exchange of business plans and strategies, which would assist in clarification of the strategic goals of each and hence alignment of goals. An exchange of strategic information would then facilitate the process of producing a strategic plan together. The survey probed some of these aspects of strategic planning in the context of KAM relationships, as shown in Figure 5.10.

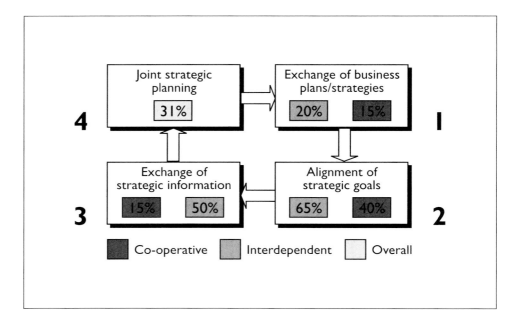

Exchange of business plans/strategies

Exchange of information on business plans and strategies is very limited, with the parties to interdependent relationships being only slightly better informed than those in co-operative relationships, and only a fifth of the former were sharing information freely or extensively on this subject. The conclusion must be that even when joint strategic planning does occur, the process rarely seems to start at this point.

Alignment of strategic goals

In co-operative relationships, feeling was equally divided between those who thought that their own goals were very different from their partners' and those who thought they were not. Given the limited exposure they have to what those goals are, it may be that this judgement is not particularly well informed anyway. Nevertheless, they may reach such an interpretation through their various dealings together, and it may be that a sub- or semi-conscious conflict of strategic goals could keep the relationship at this level and prevent it from developing further. This view may reveal a fundamental approach to business which does not really espouse relationship marketing at a more than superficial level, and will keep these companies at arm's length indefinitely.

The feeling in interdependent relationships is different: a majority of these companies believe that strategic goals do not have to be different, and presumably that alignment of goals and working towards the same objectives can happen, in theory at least.

Exchange of 'strategic' information

The survey did not address the point in these terms. However, sharing of marketing research information has been taken to mean this type of information, although the issue of exactly what other kind of strategic information is exchanged would certainly bear further investigation. Using marketing research as an indicator, sharing was indeed very limited, even though it would be a useful and potentially less sensitive input to the planning process than actual business plans. Companies with interdependent relationships might get a glimpse of buying company strategy through involvement in product/service development. This kind of information was freely exchanged in three-quarters of these relationships, but much less so in co-operative relationships.

Joint strategic planning

The measure on joint strategic planning formed part of the characterisation of the relationship stages and therefore should not be reported as an independent variable. It would be likely to follow the pattern of difference established between the two relationships, however. In relationships judged by success rather than by relationship stage, nearly half of relationships rated as successful were involved in joint strategic planning, while only one in five of the others were.

Figure 5.10 illustrates the difference between the two types of relationship, showing that there are generally more of the constituent processes occurring in interdependent relationships than there are in co-operative ones. Highest levels of occurrence lie with the chance of aligning strategic goals, which is less of a process than an admission of a possibility. Otherwise, evidence of this kind of planning process in co-operative relationships is not common.

A number of barriers to strategic planning exist, but where it does occur, it is at least linked with perceptions of success. Strategic planning preparation seems to surface in the middle of the process mapped out above, with alignment of strategic goals perhaps based on instinct rather than explicit discussion, and then moving on to joint development of plans in some cases. The evidence seems to suggest that a proper bedrock of mutual understanding is rarely laid down in terms of shared, strategically relevant information and transparent strategies.

A proper bedrock of mutual understanding is rarely laid down in terms of shared, strategically-relevant information and transparent strategies.

In interdependent relationships, more of the ingredients are present for strategic planning to take place than in co-operative relationships. There is every incentive to do so, because these are the relationships where the parties are more comfortable with each other, where they can plan joint development because they expect a longer-lasting relationship, where they can exceed their individual capabilities and streamline their processes by working together.

At the same time, these are the relationships where partners can get so comfortable together that they lose sight of their objectives, where the business is so important that they are too nervous of the consequences to take action even when squeezed too much by their partner, where the offer delivered has become so complex that it is not properly costed and monitored and may well cost more than the relationship earns.

The survey showed that interdependent relationships were less rigorously monitored than co-operative ones, which may demonstrate greater trust, but probably shows the difficulties of measuring and allocating cost fully, mixed with a certain amount of unwillingness to do so. After all, revealing that a company's most important customers or suppliers are unprofitable or expensive will not reflect well on the key person involved in management of the relationship. If that is the case, greater controls and leaner practices are likely to be imposed, which may discomfit that key contact both directly and also indirectly, as the one who bears the news to the relationship partner and implements the new regime.

Co-operative relationships appear to be almost excluded from any possibility of joint strategic planning.

Co-operative relationships appear to be almost excluded from any possibility of joint strategic planning. They do not have much information to work with, and if they are just one among many such relationships, neither the buying company's purchasing manager nor even the selling company's key account manager is likely to give this kind of relationship a great deal of time and attention, especially if long-term relationship development planning is not their style anyway.

It becomes a self-fulfilling prophecy that the relationship will continue at this level or even decline unless strenuous effort is applied, probably on the part of the selling company, to make a difference. At the same time, where the amount of attention received by a relationship is so rationed, it should not be soaking up large amounts of unattributed costs and may actually be more profitable than out-of-control interdependent relationships.

Only if one or other party, or both, targets the relationship as being of strategic importance is it going to develop: passage of time does not make a relationship evolve of itself. That will require effort invested in planning a strategy and further effort and money devoted to implementing it, which comes back to the importance of being selective and objective in singling out relationships for development.

In summary, there are both incentives and barriers to better strategic planning in KAM relationships, and plenty of scope for improvement.

5.7 TRUST

Expression of trust in KAM relationships

A degree of trust is fundamental in the development of any kind of relationship, commercial, social or personal. At the beginning of a relationship, there are many kinds of risk potentially associated with it. The participants do not know whether they can believe in each other's intentions; whether they can rely on fulfilment of those intentions; whether as new requirements or problems develop, each will adapt readily and willingly; whether each will be consistent and constant over an extended period of time.

Prudence will generally be exercised in a commercial relationship because the health of the company and the career of the individual are both tied up in its success. Trust can develop when participants in a relationship perceive a sufficiently reduced level of risk associated with it. Their perception will be formed by a combination of experience and expectation, with expectation being dominant in the early days, until a significant amount of experience is gained. Eventually, the relative importance of the two elements will presumably settle down to a fairly stable mix.

Demonstration of trust can take a number of forms:

- *sharing of 'secrets'*: imparting exclusive or commercially sensitive information;

- *relaxation of monitoring*: confidence in consistently excellent performance;

Passage of time does not make a relationship evolve of itself.

Trust can develop when participants in a relationship perceive a sufficiently reduced level of risk associated with it.

- *dedication to the relationship partner*: here, commitment of all, or a critical amount, of a purchase category or supply capability;

- *dissociation from possible alternatives*: renunciation of shopping around and flirting with competitors.

Sharing of 'secrets'

Certain kinds of information are necessary to run trading efficiently, and IT now allows much easier access to it. The information most readily shared appears to be the basics: stock availability, product/service specification and sales (total and mutual). However, even on these elements exchange was 'free' or 'extensive' between only half of companies in co-operative relationships. Although the IT capability must now be there to access the data, information is still rationed at this level. There could be a number of reasons, lack of time being one of them, but lack of trust is very likely to be an important factor, particularly when compared with the higher levels of exchange in interdependent KAM relationships.

The large difference observed in levels of exchange on product/service development makes this look like a strong indicator of the development of trust. As companies strive to arrive in the marketplace with a new idea ahead of their rivals, they are generally very careful about divulging information in case it might leak to competitors. Ideally, suppliers should be part of the development process, but often they are not, at least until the relationship has developed beyond co-operative KAM.

Relaxation of monitoring

If a buying company elected to relax its monitoring of particular suppliers, it would no doubt be a clear indication of trust, but also poor business management. The information is required for more uses than individual supplier performance assessment alone. New methodologies in supply chain management, supported by developments in IT, have increased monitoring capabilities in many respects.

In theory, companies should welcome the opportunity to prove their value to their trading partner. Whether they genuinely do or not, comprehensive monitoring of a relationship's performance has been made more difficult by global relationships, greater variation in trading arrangements, matrix structures and pressure to improve customer support packages, among other factors. The survey showed a range of degrees of monitoring in both co-operative and interdependent relationships. Monitoring of co-operative relationships seemed more extensive, but whether because it is just more difficult in complex interdependent relationships, or whether because sufficient trust has developed to allow the buyer to relax their vigilance, is a subject for further research.

Dedication to the relationship partner

Considerably more selling companies in interdependent relationships had secured a higher share of the buying company's purchases than those in co-operative relationships. However, there will always be some at any relationship stage who have gained a high share of a purchase category, not because they are well trusted, but because it does not make logistical or commercial sense to dual-source, and so the buying company has decided to accept the risk (while no doubt minimising it in other ways). In fact, it may be this necessity which has naturally drawn the relationship closer, rather than the closeness of the relationship preceding and promoting the development of the business.

Dissociation from possible alternatives

It seems that trust in commercial relationships has its limitations, which include giving up flirting with, or at least checking out, the competition to the selling company. With just a few exceptions, nobody on either side of the relationship thinks it is otherwise. Competitor monitoring may well be more about keeping the selling company on its toes than any genuine threat of switching. The individual buyer may also need to protect the perception of his or her professionalism and integrity, particularly within the buying company.

Indeed, most buyers have experience of selling companies that absorb savings into their own margins for as long as possible and do not invariably pass them on to the buying company, or that elect to lag behind in investment in new technology until their customers insist upon it. Therefore the buyer feels bound to maintain pressure in some way, checking on costs and new ideas. Cessation of competitor monitoring may be the litmus test of an integrated relationship, though it cannot be asserted from this survey as only one was encountered. Monitoring demonstrates that buying companies still see a clear separation between themselves and their supplier.

*The company's
system of
accountability ...
is the main driver
for individuals and
the relationships
they manage.*

Commercial relationships are essentially different from personal ones. Confidence in performance and professional integrity should form the basis of trust in these relationships, and the kind of blind faith that may be encountered at a personal level is, and should be, a rarity in business. However, in reality, commercial relationships are not run on an entirely objective and commercial basis either. Personal preferences and limitations and personal agendas enter into them as well.

In theory the goals of the business should be the commercial considerations that drive employee behaviour, but it is more likely that the company's system of accountability, put in place to protect itself from gullibility and rashness as well as knavery, is the main driver for individuals and the relationships they manage. In this context, the manifestation and role of trust in relationships with external partners is complex and multifaceted.

6

Conclusions

6.1 MAIN POINTS

Applicability

This study has confirmed quantitatively some elements of the existing understanding of key account relationships which had been developed from qualitative research. Such confirmation adds to confidence that those elements are widely applicable across a range of sectors and approaches to business, not just in the more limited number of companies previously researched.

Relationship characterisation

One of the purposes of this research was the design of a 'test' which could be readily applied to determine the stage of development reached in any individual key relationship. The six-parameter test used here seems to work effectively in relationship characterisation, as judged by observing other aspects of the behaviour of each of two categories of relationship, co-operative and interdependent, in terms of logic and the observations of other authors.

New labels

The new relationship names proposed here offer improvements as descriptors of the relationship itself, which then allows them to be used by both buying and selling companies without being inappropriate in either case. It is recommended that they be generally adopted in order to assist closer dialogue between selling companies and buying companies, which could advance the cause of better understanding between the two sides and perhaps promote a merging of the disciplines of Key Account Management and supply chain management, to the benefit of both.

Relationship success

A link was found between development of the relationship and perception of the relationship's success, albeit not a simple one. In two-thirds of cases, higher perceptions of success were associated with interdependent rather than co-operative relationships. However, a substantial minority does not conform to this 'rule', and where the relationship is unsophisticated and successful it may well be quite adequate and yield a good return to both parties. Relationships that are sophisticated, and therefore probably incur extra expenses, and also unsuccessful should obviously be investigated.

Interdependent relationships were also shown to be more successful than co-operative ones if measured in terms of the buying company's category spend. Successful relationships were characterised by a spirit of partnership and higher levels of joint strategic planning, which was otherwise not commonly in force. This research could not determine which is 'cause' and which is 'effect', however.

Single point of contact

Respondents reported that several key account managers worked in the same customer in half of these cases, with a third being visited by salespeople from other group companies. The conclusion is that one of the principles of Key Account Management, that of full co-ordination and account responsibility through one single point of contact for the customer, is still often not fulfilled.

Leveraging access to development

Access to product/service development was found to be an important difference between interdependent and co-operative relationships: the more involved selling companies can make much of this advantage. It allows them to be at the forefront of market-led developments, to design out cost and to design in specifications in ways which suit their capabilities and keep competitors even further on the outside, and it gives them more opportunities to broaden their constituency within the customer's organisation. Selling companies in co-operative relationships are to a greater extent 'out in the cold' and 'in the dark'.

Customer profitability

The main conclusion to be drawn appears to be that advancing the relationship is to be recommended, but a note of caution should be sounded. Although response was low in the relevant part of this survey, the findings are amply corroborated elsewhere, that close customer relationships can be a 'poisoned apple'. The business may be secured at the cost of gaining a profit from it: the customer can, wittingly or unwittingly, absorb so much in extra services that, when taken together with the prices they have used their position to leverage, they become a loss-making area of business. Very careful analysis and management of these relationships is clearly indicated.

New approaches

Several models are presented to aid visualisation of certain aspects of KAM relationships, some of them modifications of previous concepts adapted to the KAM environment. For example, Maslow's pyramid of the hierarchy of human needs can be equated to the hierarchy of needs of the parties to the relationship: at base, efficient transactions, with further development being built up progressively, without abandoning any of them.

In addition to the new labels on the stages of development, a neutral title for the discipline of key relationship management, acceptable to both buyers and sellers, would also be useful to promote an impartial approach. This study has sought to advance the mutual understanding of buyer/seller relationships, which are double-sided phenomena. As Confucius said, 'What is the sound of one hand clapping?'

6.2 NEXT STAGE OF RESEARCH

Challenges for the future

The challenge for the future is the ever-increasing scope of Key Account Management, and the globalisation of supply chains and how to organise them. Apart from the complexity of multidimensional reporting lines, integrating the business processes of the two parties to the relationship is normally a massive task. Information systems are integral to streamlining processes and ensuring communication and efficiency, but automating without understanding is fraught with opportunities for failure.

The research project presented herein has put some useful 'pegs in the ground', identifying key factors in relationship development and supporting and questioning more intellectual and speculative work. However, the methodology is not able to deal with high levels of complexity, nor is it able to pick up signs of excellent practice and future developments. The next stage of research is designed to further understanding of good practice and the processes that deliver it, and to identify ways forward for companies rather than reporting on the current position.

Framework for new research

The framework of six topics for investigation is as follows.

Selecting and prioritising key relationships, and targeting relationship development

Most companies' selection processes are rudimentary and do not even reflect their behaviour towards relationships in many cases. Nevertheless, there are examples of excellent practice around in terms of prioritising key relationships, but research should trace through this objective evaluation into actual management.

Relationship profitability

The role of finance and information systems needs to be examined in building buyer/seller relationships. Few organisations appear to understand the real costs of dealing with major accounts, and systems are not in place for evaluating, monitoring and building shareholder value. There is a need to understand sources of cost/loss and organisational factors, however, before proceeding to build large systems with adequate analytical capability.

Analysis of key accounts and strategic planning

This research has demonstrated the low incidence of strategic planning in these accounts, even though they may have been designated those on which the company's survival hangs. Research should identify good working practice where it is valued by both buying and selling companies, and understand the barriers to implementing what is a fairly normal procedure in other business areas.

Organisation and barriers in key relationship management

There are far-reaching organisational implications of customer value creation across functional boundaries. The impact on traditional structures and processes is likely to encounter opposition from the 'barons' at the top through to the implementers at the bottom unless key issues are handled from the beginning. Research to date has illustrated the problems but is unclear on good solutions.

People: recruitment and rewards, and skills, training and leadership

The human resource issues arising from the new skill sets required of key account managers and their counterparts at strategic and operational levels, and at different stages in the relationship model, need to be investigated. Buyers expect the key account manager to wield a high level of authority, which entails a high status in the selling company.

Key relationship management processes

The foregoing should lead to a set of deliverables in the form of models, processes, systems, procedures and guidelines, there being little point in research for its own sake.

Multi-function, multi-level research

Cranfield's 1996 research project investigated pairs of buying and selling companies in order to gain the breadth and objectivity required to give genuine guidance. This next stage will pursue that principle further, by including functions adjacent to key relationship management and also people at different levels in the organisation. The sample will consist of eight buyer/seller dyads drawn from a balanced range of market situations to ensure that the influence of the market can be seen, understood, and interpreted and generalised where desirable. Figure 6.1 shows the anticipated spread of participating buyer/seller dyads, in terms of market situation and offer differentiation, which will represent a range of relative buyer versus seller power balances.

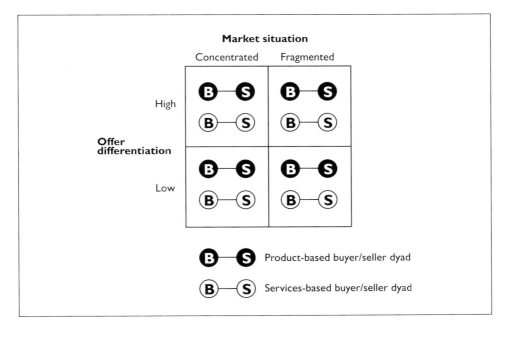

FIGURE 6.1

Sample structure for next stage of research

This next stage of research through interviewing will be augmented by the involvement of members of the Cranfield Key Account Management Best Practice Club. Delegates, all from world-leading companies across a wide range of sectors, will be amplifying findings from the external research, providing insights into areas where external participants may be unwilling to share, and testing conceptual models as the project develops them.

The agenda for growing understanding of good key relationships management is very full, but no less than companies seek.

Appendices

Description of sample

A.1 INDUSTRY SECTOR

Respondents were given a list of ten industry sectors and asked to indicate to which their companies belonged (sectors were clearly distinguished from role, e.g. manufacturer, service provider, which were examined in a separate question). The sample represented a good spread of sectors, covering both business-to-business and consumer companies (*see* Figure A.1). The largest number fell into the 'other business services' sector which is not genuine clustering but rather highlights the difficulty of classifying the multitude of business services.

FIGURE A.1

Sector breakdown of sample (number: base = 37)

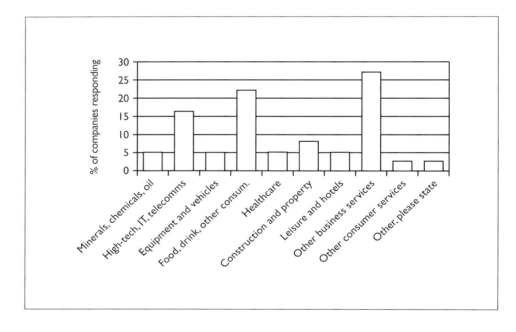

A.2 ROLE IN MARKET

Figure A.2 shows the breakdown of the sample in terms of role, as manufacturer or distributor, of products or services. Approaching half of the sample claimed to be manufacturers, and the companies handling a physical product at some point outweighed services companies by 3 : 1. There appeared to be no distributors of services in the sample, but probably because the distinction between service origination and distribution is largely academic and not recognised in reality. A minority of the sample, 5 out of 37, were retailers to consumers.

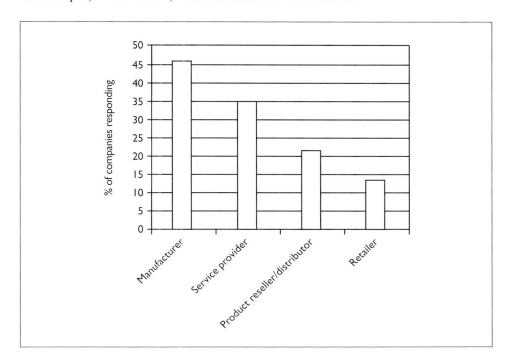

Figure A.2

**Role in market
(number: base = 37)**

A.3 ROLE IN SURVEY

Sixteen companies responded as sellers, reflecting 47 relationships with key customers from the selling point of view. (They were asked to describe their three largest accounts.)

Twenty-one companies responded as buyers, reflecting 42 relationships with key suppliers from the buying point of view. (Anticipating a lower level of interest in the survey subject from the buying side, they were asked to describe their two largest suppliers.)

Job titles are important in confirming that appropriate people are responding to the questions asked. Pre-qualifaction by telephone helped to ensure that this was the case. Over half of respondents appeared to hold board-level or equivalent positions, and the remainder held senior management jobs which were directly relevant to the topic. The breakdown is shown below:

Job title	No. of respondents
Director or vice president	14
Other titles apparently at equivalent level	6
Managers	15
Not clear	2
Total	37

A.4 COMPANY SIZE

For reasons given earlier, companies with a turnover less than £50 m p.a. were excluded from the survey unless they were part of a larger company (when relevant company size is an ambiguous point). Bearing this ambiguity in mind, size as determined by turnover was fairly evenly spread between those with a turnover of under £200 m p.a. and those with a turnover of over £200 m p.a. (*see* Figure A.3).

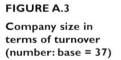

FIGURE A.3

Company size in terms of turnover (number: base = 37)

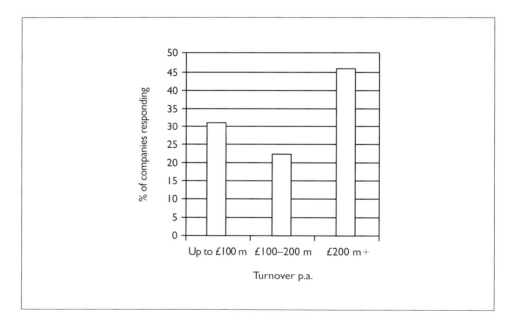

A.5 COMPANY CONSTITUTION

The majority of the sample were subsidiaries within a company group, and over three-quarters were part of a group or the head office for the group. Only a small number, 6 out of 37, were independent companies (*see* Table A.1).

Company constitution	No. in sample Base = 37
No reply	0
Independent company	6
Head office for group of companies	8
Subsidiary within group of companies	22
Other, please state	3

TABLE A.1

Constitution of sample companies

A.6 MARKET LEADERSHIP

Over a quarter of the companies in the sample held market shares of over 40 per cent, and over half of the sample were brand leaders in their core markets (*see* Table A.2). As companies with strong market positions and recognised leaders, examples of good practice across many processes could be expected from them.

Market position	No. in sample Base = 37
Market share in core markets	
No reply	4
0–9%	4
10–19%	10
20–29%	4
30–39%	5
40%+	10
Brand leadership	
No reply	5
Yes	18
No	14

TABLE A.2

Market share and brand leadership

Analytical framework

B.1 SCORING PROCESS

The two surveys were merged for most purposes and questions analysed according to three main breakdowns: viewpoint (whether from a buying or a selling company); relationship stage reached (*see* B.2); and perception of success (*see* B.3).

Viewpoint was simply recorded by the respondent. The other parameters were assessed through a scoring process described below. Additional scores were used where a set of questions was grouped around the same theme; these are also shown below.

In reality, assessment on any aggregated parameter is represented by a continuum of scores, not a single point, and therefore replies are allocated according to a range based around the 'typical' score.

B.2 STAGE OF RELATIONSHIP

The scale of relationship stage reached was calibrated by modelling the responses of relationships representing each stage of development as shown in Table B.1. Answers were scored on a scale of 1 to 5:

1 = response very negative to a close, well-developed relationship

2 = response quite negative to a close, well-developed relationship

3 = neither positive nor negative

4 = response quite positive to a close, well-developed relationship

5 = response very positive to a close, well-developed relationship

In order to prevent habitual patterns of completion, some of the statements were formulated in a negative sense, relative to good relationships. They were then scored in reverse (i.e. competitor monitoring, social association).

Statement subject	Scoring				
	1	2	3	4	5
Mutual dependency	*Strongly disagree* Basic	*Disagree* Co-operative	*Neither* Co-operative	*Agree* Interdependent	*Strongly agree* Integrated
Competitor monitoring	*Strongly agree* Basic	*Agree* Co-operative	*Neither* Interdependent	*Disagree* Integrated	*Strongly disagree* Integrated
Attitude	*Strongly disagree* Basic	*Disagree* Basic	*Neither* Co-operative	*Agree* Interdependent	*Strongly agree* Integrated
Cross-functional teams	*Strongly disagree* Basic	*Disagree* Basic	*Neither* Co-operative	*Agree* Interdependent	*Strongly agree* Integrated
Social association	*Strongly agree* Basic	*Agree* Basic	*Neither* Co-operative	*Disagree* Interdependent	*Strongly disagree* Integrated
Long-term strategic approach	*Strongly disagree* Basic	*Disagree* Co-operative	*Neither* Interdependent	*Agree* Interdependent	*Strongly agree* Integrated
Total score	6–9	15/16	22/23	29/30	
Range	6–11	12–18	19–25	26–30	
Title	Basic	Co-operative	Interdependent	Integrated	

NB: Exploratory KAM is not shown as this stage was effectively ruled out by asking for information on the two or three existing largest customers/suppliers. Disintegrating KAM is not included either as it is not a single stage but a decline from any of the others; scoring on this basis is therefore inappropriate.

The normal five-point Likert scale needed to be used to characterise the four stages of KAM relationships identified in previous research (McDonald, Millman and Rogers, 1996). Table B.1 shows how this was done, making certain assumptions based on previous research (*see* Chapter 2) and experience. It attempts to recognise that different factors are likely to come into operation at different points in the relationship. In fact, given that relationships are allocated to a range of scores, the effect of any such assumptions is minimal, and is really a minor refinement in the scoring process.

B.3 SUCCESS OF RELATIONSHIP

In the same way as the development of the relationship was assessed in the section above, the relationship's success was judged (*see* Table B.2). Question 16 offered a set of statements about indications of success (*see* section 4.2 for full statements).

TABLE B.2

Modelling of scores for KAM success

Statement subject	Scoring				
	1	2	3	4	5
Financial	Strongly disagree	Disagree	Neither	Agree	Strongly agree
Operational efficiency	Strongly disagree	Disagree	Neither	Agree	Strongly agree
Strategic alignment	Strongly agree	Agree	Neither	Disagree	Strongly disagree
Ease of doing business	Strongly agree	Agree	Neither	Disagree	Strongly disagree
Sustainability	Strongly disagree	Disagree	Neither	Agree	Strongly agree
Ultimate judgement	Strongly disagree	Disagree	Neither	Agree	Strongly agree
Total score	6	12	18	24	30
Range	6–8	9–14	15–20	21–26	27–30
Title	Very poor	Quite poor	Neither poor nor good	Quite good	Very good

B.4 SUFFICIENCY OF CONTACT

Tables B.3–5 show the scoring process for overall sufficiency of contact, exchange of information and adaptation of the offer. In overall sufficiency of contact the two extreme categories did not operate as intended so the scale was contracted from a 5-point to a 3-point scale, which covered the relatively few responses at the extremes anyway.

TABLE B.3

Modelling of scores on sufficiency of contact

Contact point	Scoring				
	1	1	2	3	3
Purchasing manager/ main contact	Not at all	Not nearly enough	Not quite enough	Enough	Yes, too much
Order processing/ logistics	Not at all	Not nearly enough	Not quite enough	Enough	Yes, too much
Production/technical	Not at all	Not nearly enough	Not quite enough	Enough	Yes, too much
R&D	Not at all	Not nearly enough	Not quite enough	Enough	Yes, too much
Marketing and sales	Not at all	Not nearly enough	Not quite enough	Enough	Yes, too much
Directors	Not at all	Not nearly enough	Not quite enough	Enough	Yes, too much
Total score	6		12	18	
Range	6–9		10–14	15–18	
Title	Not nearly enough		Not quite enough	Enough	

Subject of information	Scoring					TABLE B.4
	1	2	3	4	5	**Modelling of scores on exchange of information**
Product/service specification	Not at all	Occasionally	Selectively	Extensively	Freely	
Product/service development	Not at all	Occasionally	Selectively	Extensively	Freely	
Stock/service availability	Not at all	Occasionally	Selectively	Extensively	Freely	
Sales (total and mutual)	Not at all	Occasionally	Selectively	Extensively	Freely	
Marketing research	Not at all	Occasionally	Selectively	Extensively	Freely	
Business plans and strategies	Not at all	Occasionally	Selectively	Extensively	Freely	
Costs	Not at all	Occasionally	Selectively	Extensively	Freely	
Total score	7	14	21	28	35	
Range	7–10	11–17	18–24	25–31	32–35	
Title	Not at all	Occasionally	Selectively	Extensively	Freely	

Element of offer adapted	Scoring					TABLE B.5
	1	2	3	4	5	**Modelling of scores on adaptation of the selling company offer**
Core product/service	Not at all	A little	Significantly	Quite a lot	Largely	
Extra non-core services	Not at all	A little	Significantly	Quite a lot	Largely	
Logistics	Not at all	A little	Significantly	Quite a lot	Largely	
Information supply	Not at all	A little	Significantly	Quite a lot	Largely	
Billing and paperwork	Not at all	A little	Significantly	Quite a lot	Largely	
Marketing	Not at all	A little	Significantly	Quite a lot	Largely	
Payment/finance	Not at all	A little	Significantly	Quite a lot	Largely	
Total score	7	14	21	28	35	
Range	7–10	11–17	18–24	25–31	32–35	
Title	Not at all	Occasionally	Selectively	Extensively	Freely	

Questionnaires
Research Project – Key Account Management

QUESTIONNAIRE FOR SELLING COMPANIES

Thank you for agreeing to participate in this research project, which seeks to establish some facts about KAM relationships between buying and selling companies.

All information will be kept strictly confidential, and no individual or company will be identifiable in the final report.

The questionnaire is based very largely on your company's view of the relationship, and takes about **25 minutes** to complete.

In return, you will receive a copy of the report early in 1998. We suggest you keep a copy of your own responses to compare with the results in the report.

The questionnaire has a modular form so that you can distribute relevant parts to colleagues if appropriate.

We are very grateful for your help.

All participants will receive the final report on Key Account Management.

Please return this questionnaire by

A reply-paid envelope is enclosed for your use. Please send your questionnaire to:

Diana Woodburn
PO Box 471
Chesham
Bucks HP5 1BR

If you need clarification or have any other queries while completing the questionnaire, please call Diana at The Marketing Process Company on 01628 662767.

Please change any incorrect or incomplete details below.

Name

Position

Company

Tel   Fax

ABOUT YOUR MOST IMPORTANT CUSTOMER (A)

*   Repeated for second and third most important customers (B) and (C)

1   Which best describes your largest customer's situation on decisions about selection of major suppliers? (largest in terms of sales turnover with you)

Independent company, unambiguous decision point	❏
Group with Central Office deciding for several subsidiaries	❏
Subsidiary deciding from given supplier short list	❏
Subsidiary deciding independently	❏
Other (please state)	❏

Please base your answers to the following questions on the customer defined by your answer to Q1

2   Which customer is your largest Key Account, in terms of sales volume? (£pa)

Company

How long have you been dealing with this customer? (years)

3 How far geographically can/does your relationship with this customer extend?

	Nowhere else	Elsewhere in UK only	Abroad mostly Europe	Abroad mostly outside Europe	World wide
They have companies buying same product/ service in these areas	❏	❏	❏	❏	❏
We can supply in these areas	❏	❏	❏	❏	❏
We already supply them or their sister cos in these areas	❏	❏	❏	❏	❏

4 How many Key Account Managers work on this customer's account?

From your company

From other companies in your group

Not applicable: no other cos in group

5 Do your customer's people have sufficient contact with the following people in your own company?

	Yes, too much	Enough	Not quite enough	Not nearly enough	Not at all
Purchasing Mgr/main contact	❏	❏	❏	❏	❏
Order processing/ logistics	❏	❏	❏	❏	❏
Production/technical	❏	❏	❏	❏	❏
R & D	❏	❏	❏	❏	❏
Marketing & sales	❏	❏	❏	❏	❏
Directors	❏	❏	❏	❏	❏

6 To what extent is there a two-way exchange of information with this customer?

	Freely	Extensively	Selectively	Occasionally	Not at all
Product/service specification	❏	❏	❏	❏	❏
Product/service development	❏	❏	❏	❏	❏
Stocks/service availability	❏	❏	❏	❏	❏

	Strongly agree	Agree	Neither agree nor disagree	Disagree	Strongly disagree
Sales (total & mutual)	❏	❏	❏	❏	❏
Marketing research	❏	❏	❏	❏	❏
Business plans & strategies	❏	❏	❏	❏	❏
Costs	❏	❏	❏	❏	❏

7 To what extent do you agree or disagree with the following statements, applied to your relationship with this customer?

	Strongly agree	Agree	Neither agree nor disagree	Disagree	Strongly disagree
"If either company (we or our customer) ever wanted to end our relationship, both companies would find it difficult and complicated to exit."	❏	❏	❏	❏	❏
"We keep our relationships with the people in this customer's organisation strictly on a business footing: we don't meet outside work."	❏	❏	❏	❏	❏
"They still monitor competitors regularly to check up on our performance."	❏	❏	❏	❏	❏
"There is a real spirit of partnership between our two companies."	❏	❏	❏	❏	❏
"Looking after this customer is not just the responsibility of the Key Account Manager: both companies have set up cross-functional teams of people dedicated to meeting their needs."	❏	❏	❏	❏	❏
"Together we have planned and formally documented long-term strategies for the development of our relationship."	❏	❏	❏	❏	❏

8 What does this customer buy from you?

9   For what purpose does this customer buy this product/service?

For resale, with or without adding value   ❏

For own use within business   ❏

10 How would you describe the nature of the product/service you sell to this customer?

Very complex   ❏

Quite complex   ❏

Neither complex nor simple   ❏

Quite simple   ❏

Very simple   ❏

11 What level of support from your company do these purchases require?

	Very high	Quite high	Neither high nor low	Quite low	Very low
Selling & pre-introduction	❏	❏	❏	❏	❏
At introduction/ installation	❏	❏	❏	❏	❏
Throughout lifetime of use/resale	❏	❏	❏	❏	❏

12 To what extent have different aspects of your standard offer been adapted to meet this customer's specific needs?

	Not at all	A little	Significantly	Quite a lot	Largely
Core product/service	❏	❏	❏	❏	❏
Extra non-core services	❏	❏	❏	❏	❏
Logistics	❏	❏	❏	❏	❏
Information supply	❏	❏	❏	❏	❏
Billing & paperwork	❏	❏	❏	❏	❏
Marketing	❏	❏	❏	❏	❏
Payment/finance	❏	❏	❏	❏	❏

13 Customer value

How much does this customer buy from you? (as £pa)
_____

What gross margin does that represent? (as £pa)
_____

After deduction of attributable sales & other support services cost, what contribution remains? (£pa)
_____

14 To what extent do you quantify & allocate costs of all the support services this customer receives?

Completely ❏

Largely ❏

Partly ❏

Not really ❏

Not at all ❏

15 What share of this customer's budget do you estimate you have for:

	Under 10%	10–24%	25–49%	50–75%	Over 75%
products/services of this type	❏	❏	❏	❏	❏
all products/services they buy for resale OR for business improvement (whichever, Q9)	❏	❏	❏	❏	❏

16 To what extent do you agree or disagree with the following statements, applied to your relationship with this customer?

	Agree strongly	Agree	Neither agree nor disagree	Disagree	Strongly disagree
"We are very happy with the financial return we get on this customer's business."	❏	❏	❏	❏	❏
"Our operational processes (order handling, logistics, documentation etc.) work seamlessly and cost-effectively with this customer."	❏	❏	❏	❏	❏
"Our own strategic goals are very different from this customer's strategic goals."	❏	❏	❏	❏	❏
"This customer is rather inflexible and/or disorganised so it is not easy to do business with them."	❏	❏	❏	❏	❏

"Our relationship with this customer must be one of the longest in the sector."	❏	❏	❏	❏	❏
"Our Managing Director (or equivalent) rates the business with this customer as extremely successful and one of the most important to us strategically."	❏	❏	❏	❏	❏

17 Of the following, which best describes your customer's industry sector? (Please tick only one)

Minerals, chemicals, oil	❏
High-tech, IT, telecomms	❏
Equipment & vehicles	❏
Food, drink, other consumer goods	❏
Healthcare	❏
Construction & property	❏
Leisure & hotels	❏
Financial services	❏
Other business services	❏
Other consumer services	❏

18 Which of the following best describes your customer's role in their market?

Manufacturer	❏
Product reseller/distributor	❏
Product retailer	❏
Service provider	❏
Service reseller	❏
Service retailer	❏

19 Which of the following best describes the situation in your customer's core markets?

	Very high	Quite high	Not high nor low	Quite low	Very low/nil	Don't know
Competitive intensity	❏	❏	❏	❏	❏	❏
Market growth	❏	❏	❏	❏	❏	❏
Rate of innovation	❏	❏	❏	❏	❏	❏
Average margins	❏	❏	❏	❏	❏	❏
Uncertainty	❏	❏	❏	❏	❏	❏

20   Overall, how does your company view the prospects in your customer's core markets?

Excellent ❏

Good ❏

Neither good nor poor ❏

Poor ❏

Very poor ❏

Don't know ❏

ABOUT YOUR COMPANY

21   Within your organisation, what does your company represent?

Independent company ❏

Head Office for group of companies ❏

Subsidiary within group of companies ❏

Other, please state ❏

Please answer the following questions for your company as defined above.

22   Of the following, which best describes your company's industry sector? (Please tick only one)

Minerals, chemicals, oil ❏

High-tech, IT, telecomms ❏

Equipment & vehicles ❏

Food, drink, other consumer goods ❏

Healthcare ❏

Construction & property ❏

Leisure & hotels ❏

Financial services ❏

Other business services ❏

Other consumer services ❏

23   What are your core products/services?

24   Which of the following best describes your role in your market?

Manufacturer   ❑

Product reseller/distributor   ❑

Product retailer   ❑

Service provider   ❑

Service reseller   ❑

Service retailer   ❑

25   Which of the following best describes the situation in your core markets?

	Very high	Quite high	Neither high nor low	Quite low	Very low/nil
Competitive intensity	❑	❑	❑	❑	❑
Market growth	❑	❑	❑	❑	❑
Rate of innovation	❑	❑	❑	❑	❑
Average margins	❑	❑	❑	❑	❑
Uncertainty	❑	❑	❑	❑	❑

26   Overall, how does your company view the prospects in your core markets?

Excellent   ❑

Good   ❑

Neither good nor poor   ❑

Poor   ❑

Very poor   ❑

27   Company size

What is your company's total sales turnover? (in £pa)

What is your average gross margin % across
all products and customers?

Are you generally brand leader in terms of market share? (Yes/No)

What is your average market share in your core markets?

28   Key customers

How many customers do you classify as key to your business?

What proportion of your total sales turnover comes
from these customers? (%)

THANK YOU FOR YOUR HELP

You will have made a useful contribution to the body of knowledge on Key Account Management, and we are very grateful for your help. The results of the survey will be sent to you early in 1998.

May we contact the customers you have named here to ask them if they would like to contribute to Cranfield's research into Key Account Management? (Please note: all information you have given in this questionnaire would remain confidential.)

Yes/No

If yes, please give contact details

Company A
_____
Contact name
_____
Tel no.
_____

Company B
_____
Contact name
_____
Tel no.
_____

Company C
_____
Contact name
_____
Tel no.
_____

Are you prepared to consider participation in later stages of this project?

Yes/No

Cranfield UNIVERSITY

School of Management

QUESTIONNAIRE FOR BUYING COMPANIES

* Repeated for second most important supplier (B)

Thank you for agreeing to participate in this research project, which seeks to establish some facts about KAM relationships between buying and selling companies.

All information will be kept strictly confidential, and no individual or company will be identifiable in the final report.

The questionnaire is based very largely on your company's view of the relationship, and takes about **25 minutes** to complete.

In return, you will receive a copy of the report early in 1998. We suggest you keep a copy of your own responses to compare with the results in the report.

The questionnaire has a modular form so that you can distribute relevant parts to colleagues if appropriate.

We are very grateful for your help.

All participants will receive the final report on Key Account Management.

Please return this questionnaire by

A reply-paid envelope is enclosed for your use. Please send your questionnaire to:

Diana Woodburn
PO Box 471
Chesham
Bucks HP5 1BR

If you need clarification or have any other queries while completing the questionnaire, please call Diana at The Marketing Process Company on 01628 662767.

Please change any incorrect or incomplete details below.

Name

Position

Company

Tel   Fax

ABOUT YOUR MOST IMPORTANT SUPPLIER (A)

1   Which best describes your situation on decisions about selection of
    major suppliers?

    Independent company, unambiguous decision point   ❏

    Group with Central Office deciding for several subsidiaries ❏

    Subsidiary deciding from given supplier short list   ❏

    Subsidiary deciding independently   ❏

    Other (please state)   ❏

**Please base your answers to the following questions on your buying entity
defined by your answer to Q1**

2   Which is your most important supplier, in terms of volume of purchases? (£)

    Company

    How long have you been dealing with this supplier? (years)

3   How far geographically can/does your relationship with this supplier extend?

	Nowhere else	Elsewhere in UK only	Abroad mostly Europe	Abroad mostly outside Europe	World wide
We have cos buying same product/service in these areas	❏	❏	❏	❏	❏
They can supply in these areas	❏	❏	❏	❏	❏
They already supply us or our sister cos in these areas	❏	❏	❏	❏	❏

4   How many of your supplier's Key Account Managers work on your
    company's account?

    From your principal supply company

    From other companies in their group

    Not applicable: no other cos in their group

5   Do your supplier's people have sufficient contact with the following people in your own company?

	Yes, too much	Enough	Not quite enough	Not nearly enough	Not at all
Purchasing Mgr/main contact	❏	❏	❏	❏	❏
Order processing/ logistics	❏	❏	❏	❏	❏
Production/technical	❏	❏	❏	❏	❏
R & D	❏	❏	❏	❏	❏
Marketing & sales	❏	❏	❏	❏	❏
Directors	❏	❏	❏	❏	❏

6   To what extent is there a two-way exchange of information with this supplier?

	Freely	Extensively	Selectively	Occasionally	Not at all
Product/service specification	❏	❏	❏	❏	❏
Product/service development	❏	❏	❏	❏	❏
Stocks/service availability	❏	❏	❏	❏	❏
Sales (total & mutual)	❏	❏	❏	❏	❏
Marketing research	❏	❏	❏	❏	❏
Business plans & strategies	❏	❏	❏	❏	❏
Costs	❏	❏	❏	❏	❏

7   To what extent do you agree or disagree with the following statements, applied to your relationship with this supplier?

	Strongly agree	Agree	Neither agree nor disagree	Disagree	Strongly disagree
"If either company (we or our supplier) ever wanted to end our relationship, both companies would find it difficult and complicated to exit."	❏	❏	❏	❏	❏

"We keep our relationships with the people in this supplier's organisation strictly on a business footing: we don't meet outside work." ❑ ❑ ❑ ❑ ❑

"We still monitor competitors regularly to check up on their performance." ❑ ❑ ❑ ❑ ❑

"There is a real spirit of partnership between our two companies." ❑ ❑ ❑ ❑ ❑

"Looking after our business is not just the responsibility of the Key Account Manager: both companies have set up cross-functional teams of people dedicated to meeting our needs." ❑ ❑ ❑ ❑ ❑

"Together we have planned and formally documented long-term strategies for the development of our relationship." ❑ ❑ ❑ ❑ ❑

8 What do you buy from this supplier?

---

9 For what purpose do you buy this product/service?

For resale, with or without adding value ❑

For own use within business ❑

10 How would you describe the nature of the product/service you buy from this supplier?

Very complex ❑

Quite complex ❑

Neither complex nor simple ❑

Quite simple ❑

Very simple ❑

11   What level of support from your supplier do these purchases require?

	Very high	Quite high	Neither high nor low	Quite low	Very low
Selling & pre-introduction	❑	❑	❑	❑	❑
At introduction/ installation	❑	❑	❑	❑	❑
Throughout lifetime of use/resale	❑	❑	❑	❑	❑

12   To what extent have different aspects of your supplier's standard offer been adapted to meet your specific needs?

	Not at all	A little	Significantly	Quite a lot	Largely
Core product/service	❑	❑	❑	❑	❑
Extra non-core services	❑	❑	❑	❑	❑
Logistics	❑	❑	❑	❑	❑
Information supply	❑	❑	❑	❑	❑
Billing & paperwork	❑	❑	❑	❑	❑
Marketing	❑	❑	❑	❑	❑
Payment/finance	❑	❑	❑	❑	❑

13   Business value

How much do you buy from this supplier? (as £pa)

14   Do you have systems which measure this supplier's performance regularly and quantitatively?

Rigorously	❑
To large extent	❑
To some extent	❑
Not really	❑
Not at all	❑

15   What share has this supplier received of your budget for:

	Under 10%	10–24%	25–49%	50–75%	Over 75%
products/services of this type	❑	❑	❑	❑	❑
all products/services you buy for resale OR for business improvement (whichever, Q9)	❑	❑	❑	❑	❑

16   To what extent do you agree or disagree with the following statements, applied to your relationship with this supplier?

	Agree strongly	Agree	Neither agree nor disagree	Disagree	Strongly disagree
"We are very happy with the value we get from this supplier in financial terms."	❑	❑	❑	❑	❑
"Our operational processes (order handling, logistics, documentation etc.) work seamlessly and cost-effectively with this supplier."	❑	❑	❑	❑	❑
"Our own strategic goals are very different from this supplier's strategic goals."	❑	❑	❑	❑	❑
"This supplier is rather inflexible and/or disorganised so it is not easy to do business with them."	❑	❑	❑	❑	❑
"Our relationship with this supplier must be one of the longest in the sector."	❑	❑	❑	❑	❑
"Our Managing Director (or equivalent) rates the business with this supplier as extremely successful and one of the most important to us strategically."	❑	❑	❑	❑	❑

ABOUT YOUR COMPANY

17   Within your organisation, what does your company represent?

Independent company   ❏

Head Office for group of companies   ❏

Subsidiary within group of companies   ❏

Other, please state   ❏

Please answer the following questions for your company as defined above.

18   Of the following, which best describes your company's industry sector? (Please tick only one)

Minerals, chemicals, oil   ❏

High-tech, IT, telecomms   ❏

Equipment & vehicles   ❏

Food, drink, other consumer goods   ❏

Healthcare   ❏

Construction & property   ❏

Leisure & hotels   ❏

Financial services   ❏

Other business services   ❏

Other consumer services   ❏

19   What are your core products/services?

20   Which of the following best describes your role in your market?

Manufacturer   ❏

Product reseller/distributor   ❏

Product retailer   ❏

Service provider   ❏

Service reseller   ❏

Service retailer   ❏

21 Which of the following best describes the situation in your core markets?

	Very high	Quite high	Neither high nor low	Quite low	Very low/nil
Competitive intensity	❏	❏	❏	❏	❏
Market growth	❏	❏	❏	❏	❏
Rate of innovation	❏	❏	❏	❏	❏
Average margins	❏	❏	❏	❏	❏
Uncertainty	❏	❏	❏	❏	❏

22 Overall, how does your company view the prospects in your core markets?

Excellent ❏

Good ❏

Neither good nor poor ❏

Poor ❏

Very poor ❏

23 Company size

What is your company's total sales turnover? (in £pa)

Are you generally brand leader in terms of market share? (Yes/No)

What is your average market share in your core markets?

24 Key suppliers

How many suppliers do you classify as key to your business?

What share do the above suppliers have of your purchase budget for products/services for resale?

What share do these suppliers have of your budget for products/services for business improvement?

THANK YOU FOR YOUR HELP

You will have made a useful contribution to the body of knowledge on Key Account Management, and we are very grateful for your help. The results of the survey will be sent to you early in 1998.

May we contact the suppliers you have named here to ask them if they would like to contribute to Cranfield's research into Key Account Management? (Please note: all information you have given in this questionnaire would remain confidential.)

Yes/No

If yes, please give contact details

Company A

Contact name

Tel no.

Company B

Contact name

Tel no.

Are you prepared to consider participation in later stages of this project?

Yes/No

References

Alderson, W. (1965) *Dynamic Marketing Behaviour*. Homewood, Illinois: Richard D. Irwin Inc.

Anderson, J.C. and Narus, J.A. (1990) 'A model of distributor firm and manufacturer firm working partnerships', *Journal of Marketing*, vol. 54, pp. 42–58.

Anderson, J.C, Håkansson, H. and Johanson, J. (1994) 'Dyadic business relationships within a business network context', *Journal of Marketing*, vol. 58, pp. 1–15.

Bain Customer Retention Model (1990) *Harvard Business Review*, October.

Berry, L.L. and Parasuraman, A. (1991) *Marketing Services*. New York: Free Press.

Boles, J.S., Barksdale, H.C. and Johnson, J.T. (1996) 'What national account decision makers would tell salespeople about building relationships', *Journal of Business and Industrial Marketing*, vol. 11, no. 2, pp. 6–19.

Buchanan, D.A. and Huczynski, A.A. (1985) *Organizational Behaviour*. London: Prentice-Hall International.

Burnett, K. (1992) *Strategic Customer Alliances*. London: Pitman.

Buzzell, R.D. (1985) *Citibank: Marketing to Multinational Customers*. Boston: Harvard Business School.

Cohen, A. (1996) 'As customers demand more services and better prices, companies are increasingly adopting national account programs', *Sales and Marketing Management* (USA), no. 4, pp. 77–80.

Dunn, D.T. and Thomas, C.A. (1994) 'Partnering with customers', *Journal of Business and Industrial Marketing*, vol. 9, no. 1, pp. 34–40.

Ellram, L.E. (1991) 'Supply chain management', *International Journal of Physical Distribution and Logistics Management*, vol. 21, no.1, pp. 13–22.

Fiocca, R. (1982) 'Account portfolio analysis for strategy development', *Industrial Marketing Management*, April, pp. 53–62.

Ford, D. (1980) 'The development of buyer–seller relationships in industrial markets', *European Journal of Marketing*, vol. 14, no. 5/6, pp 339–53.

Ford, D. (ed.) (1990) *Understanding Business Markets: Interaction, Relationships and Networks*. San Diego: Academic Press.

Francis, K. (1998) 'What is a KAM?', *Winning Business*, Jan.–Mar., pp. 62–4.

Håkansson, H. (1982) *International Marketing and Purchasing of Industrial Goods: An Interactive Approach*. Chichester: John Wiley & Sons.

Krapfel, R.E., Salmond, D. and Spekman, R. (1991) 'A strategic approach to buyer–seller relationships', *European Journal of Marketing*, vol. 25, no. 9, pp. 22–37.

Lohtia, R. and Krapfel, R.E. (1994) 'The impact of transaction-specific investments on buyer–seller relationships', *Journal of Business and Industrial Marketing*, vol. 9, no. 1, pp. 6–16.

Maslow, A.H. (1943) 'A theory of human motivation', *Psychological Review*, vol. 50, no. 4, pp. 370–96.

McDonald, M., Millman, A. and Rogers, B. (1996) *Key Account Management – Learning from Supplier and Customer Perspectives*. Cranfield: Cranfield School of Management.

McDonald, M. and Rogers, B. (1998) *Key Account Management: Learning from Supplier and Customer Perspectives*. Oxford: Butterworth-Heinemann.

Millman, A. and Wilson, K. (1994) *From Key Account Selling to Key Account Management*. Tenth Annual Conference on Industrial Marketing and Purchasing, University of Groningen, The Netherlands.

Millman, A. and Wilson, K. (1996) 'Developing key account management competences', *Journal of Marketing Practice and Applied Marketing Science*, vol. 2, no. 2, pp. 7–22.

Morgan, R.M. and Hunt, S.D. (1994) 'The commitment–trust theory of relationship marketing', *Journal of Marketing*, vol. 58, pp. 20–38.

Olsen, R.F. and Ellram, L. (1997) 'Portfolio approach to supplier relations', *Industrial Marketing Management*, vol. 26, pp. 101–13.

Pardo, C., Salle, R. and Spencer, R. (1995) 'The key accountization of the firm', *Industrial Marketing Management*, vol. 22, pp. 123–43.

Pfeffer, J. and Salancik, G.R. (1978) *The External Control of Organisations: A Resource Dependence Perspective.* New York: Harper & Row.

Scott, C. and Westbrook, R. (1991) 'New strategic tools for supply chain management', *International Journal of Physical Distribution and Logistics Management*, vol. 21, no. 1, pp. 23–33.

Shapiro, B.P. (1989) *Close Encounters of the Four Kinds: Managing Customers in a Rapidly Changing Environment.* Boston: Harvard Business School.

Stevenson, T.H. (1981) 'Classifying a customer as a national account', *Industrial Marketing Management*, vol. 9, pp. 133–96.

Turnbull, P.W. and Valla, J.P. (1986) *Strategies for International Marketing.* London: Croom Helm.

Williamson, O.E. (1985) *The Economic Institution of Capitalism: Firms, Markets, Relational Contracting.* New York: Free Press.

Wilson, C. (1997) *Profitable Customers.* London: Kogan Page.

Yip, G.S. and Madsen, T.L. (1996) 'Global account management: the new frontier in relationship marketing', *International Marketing Review*, vol. 13, no. 3, pp. 24–42.

Index